11/97

D0602391

Mostly Vegetables

Stylish Recipes Celebrating the Glories
of the Vegetable Kingdom

Mostly Vegetables

Stylish Recipes Celebrating the Glories of the Vegetable Kingdom

SUSAN COSTNER

PHOTOGRAPHS BY FAITH ECHTERMEYER

BANTAM BOOKS
NEW YORK   TORONTO   LONDON   SYDNEY   AUCKLAND

MOSTLY VEGETABLES

A Bantam Book / July 1996

All rights reserved.

Copyright © 1996 by Susan Costner
Cover and interior photographs copyright © 1996 by Faith Echtermeyer
Book design by James Sinclair

No part of this book may be reproduced or transmitted in any form or by any means, electronic or
mechanical, including photocopying, recording, or by any information storage and retrieval system,
without permission in writing from the publisher.
For information address: Bantam Books.

Library of Congress Cataloging-in-Publication Data
Costner, Susan.
Mostly vegetables : stylish recipes celebrating the glories of the
vegetable kingdom / Susan Costner.
p.   cm.
Includes bibliographical references and index.
ISBN 0-553-09675-3
1. Cookery (Vegetables)   2. Vegetarian cookery.   I. Title.
TX801C67   1996
641.6′5—dc20   95-50576
CIP

Published simultaneously in the United States and Canada

Bantam Books are published by Bantam Books, a division of Bantam Doubleday Dell Publishing
Group, Inc. Its trademark, consisting of the words "Bantam Books" and the portrayal of a rooster,
is Registered in U.S. Patent and Trademark Office and in other countries. Marca Registrada.
Bantam Books, 1540 Broadway, New York, New York 10036.

PRINTED IN THE UNITED STATES OF AMERICA

FG   10   9   8   7   6   5   4   3   2   1

641.65
COS
1996

For Molly, Cooper, and Tor

My vegetable love should grow
Vaster than empires, and more slow.
—Andrew Marvell,
"To His Coy Mistress"

Acknowledgments

Every book is a collaboration, and this book owes an enormous debt to so many friends, both in the kitchen and out.

First, Kathleen Orme was an invaluable help, not only by sharing her culinary knowledge but by patiently testing and tasting all the recipes with sound feedback.

I couldn't possibly have written this book without the boundless help of Camilla Turnbull, who has assisted me with all my books from beginning to end. With such extraordinary patience and friendship, I venture to say that there isn't another person like her anywhere; some friends are forever.

I met Faith Echtermeyer 10 years ago when I first moved to Napa Valley. Over the years, as we have continued to work together, I am moved by her warmth and her talent. Of course, I can't imagine how to thank her enough.

A very special thanks to the numerous friends that contributed recipes and ideas: to Madeleine Kamman, Hubert Keller, Karen Mitchell, Julie Anne Wagner, Bruce LeFavour, the Schmitts, Lee and Wayne James, Michael Chiarello, Michelle Mutruy, Aaron Bauman, Tom Stokey, Robert Fizdale, Jerry Comfort, Gary Danko, Barbara Tropp, Jan Birnbaum, Steven Levine, and Thalia Loffredo.

Most especially I want to thank my editor, Fran McCullough, whose help and encouragement has been phenomenal. Her humor, dedication, and knowledge have been so welcoming, that I continue to marvel at my enormous good fortune to be able to work with her.

Sandy McKennery was a wonderful guide to the design of the photographs. With typical calm, she always came through, even when I called at the last minute.

As always, there is no way to thank my husband, Tor, for all of his support and for the wine suggestions. He believes and helps with each of my books in his own quiet, unassuming way, and now all he wants for dinner is vegetables.

Contents

Introduction _____

There was no single illuminating moment when I decided to assemble a collection of mostly vegetable recipes. But over a period of several years, the idea insinuated itself into my intentions in the most seductive of ways. Though I'd been an enthusiastic eater of meat all my life, I found that in cooking for family and friends what I most wanted to taste was the vegetables. Once the allure of the meal had become its accompaniments, the old main-event standbys like roast beef and leg of lamb continued to deliver what they had always delivered but no more than that; often meat seemed too filling or just too heavy for what I really wanted. But vegetables, ah . . . in their amplitude of vivid combinations, used at peak freshness and thoughtfully prepared, they were a flavor sensation, wonderfully obliging and surprisingly versatile. They were a revelation. As I came to place greater emphasis on plant-based foods, moving them front and center on the plate, I felt I had gone through a door giving onto a garden of inexhaustible earthly delights. And I wanted to share what I had found.

Today meals built around fresh produce and grains remain my single favorite thing to cook and enjoy. And yet I am not a vegetarian in any strict sense—mainly because I can't exclude any food group from my diet without immediately feeling deprived. So my approach is not doctrinaire; I have no religious, political, or nutritional reasons to go lighter on the meat dishes I used to favor. I simply prefer to eat more vegetables, grains, and fruit than meat. In fact, I like to eat *mostly* vegetables, grains, and fruit.

And I am not alone in my taste. Over the last ten years there has been a sea of change in the American diet as we seek lighter food that offers intense flavor in less time. There is a fast-growing number of Americans—over 13 million at last count—who now call themselves vegetarians and a far larger number of "near" or "part-time" vegetarians who occasionally eat chicken or fish but have adopted a diet long on vegetables, fruit, grains, legumes, pasta, bread, and dairy products. This number includes my family and a clear majority of my friends, and it even includes the federal government. Is there a cook alive who does not know of the changes in the national diet suggested by the U.S. Department of Agriculture in 1992? The Eating Right Pyramid urged us all to consume a diet consisting largely of vegetables, fruit, and whole grains for better health. No sooner was it un-

1

veiled, however, than its recommendations were challenged by a more stringent dietary model, the Traditional Healthy Mediterranean Diet Pyramid presented by the Harvard School of Public Health and the Boston-based Oldways Preservation and Exchange Trust. This plan suggested a diet with a far more sparing use of fish, poultry, eggs, and red meat.

Although the mostly vegetarian way is fashionable at the moment, it's well to remember that it is not exactly news. Thomas Jefferson, as great a plantsman as he was a statesman, attributed his long life to eating a hearty amount of vegetables and "meat as a condiment." And, of course, traditional near vegetarian diets have sustained huge populations through the millennia in such areas as Asia, India, and Latin America, often promoting long lives free of chronic disease.

The shifting of vegetables to the center of the plate is a distinctly American trend. French and Italian diners prefer their vegetables as a separate course, but here we love to see everything on the plate at once. The moment I got rid of the ubiquitous baked potato and steamed broccoli (good food, to be sure, but dull) and started cooking more inventively with a wider variety of seasonal vegetables and herbs, I found that those around my table happily eschewed meat for another serving of vegetables. And who can blame them? It's hard to resist vegetables at the height of their season—midsummer's corn and tomatoes, fall's precious hoard of wild mushrooms, the first spears of spring's tender asparagus.

As you will see, this book is not a comprehensive work on vegetable cookery, nor is it a treatise on dieting, natural foods, and nutrition, though it contains elements of these. It's simply a cookbook filled with the best vegetable recipes I know how to make. It is my first purpose to offer recipes so delicious that people who have turned "almost vegetarian" for health reasons will be persuaded by their palates that this, for them, is the most satisfying and pleasurable way to eat all the time.

In these pages you will find more than 150 stylish, cook-friendly, and predominantly quick recipes suitable for entertaining or for family dinners. Right along with them are menu-making suggestions so that you'll have an idea of what to serve with what and which wines make them sing. And this book is flexible: families eager to try meatless meals can use these menus that revolve just around vegetables. Cooks who still want to serve meat can add a roast or grilled meat or fish.

Some of the recipes do take some time to prepare, but I have included them because they just taste too good to leave out. Some recipes are purely vegetarian; some employ a little meat, poultry, or fish stocks as seasoning agents; a few have fish as the focal point. For those of you just making the switch to a more plant-based diet, using meat and poultry stocks will help in the transition, satisfying the craving for a big serving of meat without all the fat. I must confess to a preference for the traditional southern way of cooking most vegetables; bacon or chunks of seasoning meats, such as ham hocks or salt pork, were used extensively. For those wishing a lighter seasoning, I substitute pancetta because it yields less fat when rendered but adds more flavoring. I find the salty, smoky taste the perfect foil for most cooked vegetables, especially green beans and peas. Although strongly Mediterranean in focus—I live in California's Napa Valley, and our climate and growing conditions closely match those in that warm and sunny region—the recipes also incorporate flavors from the cuisines of countries such as Thailand, Mexico, China, and India, where diets have been mostly meatless for centuries. Not to mention the American South of my childhood.

You will find some surprises, too, special things I've included to serve with your vegetable courses. Fruit turns up teamed with vegetables in every section of the book, but it figures especially prominently in the desserts. These are mostly simple dishes designed to amplify the full flavor of fruit at perfect ripeness or recipes for plain cookies and easily prepared basic cakes, often fruit-based, to provide a taste of sweet at dinner's end.

I've also passed along information—and opinion—on equipment and equipment sources. It's always a pleasure to share notes on the *batterie de cuisine*. The right kitchen tool can make all the difference in the time a recipe takes and the quality of the result. For this book a good juicer is a must for the vegetable juice–based vinaigrettes and sauces; a whiz of a vegetable slicer can speed your prep work in a whole host of the recipes.

As to the matter of fresh ingredients, I note with pleasure the following comments of the great French philosopher Jean Jacques Rousseau, who in *Emile* (1762) describes what he would eat if he were rich and could have anything he wanted:

> I would always want those which are best prepared by nature and pass through the fewest hands before reaching our tables. I would prevent myself from becoming the victim of fraudulent adulteration by going

out after pleasure myself. . . . I would lavish my own efforts on the satisfaction of my own sensuality [*i.e., do his own cooking*], since then those efforts are themselves a pleasure and thus add to the pleasure one expects from them.

It is essential to use quality ingredients in these recipes. I take great pride in my vegetable garden and cannot stress enough the rewards of growing your own vegetables. For those of you with gardens, I have suggested some sources for seeds and, where pertinent, particular varieties with exceptional flavor. If you don't have space or time or just don't like gardening, make a habit of looking for the very best produce available in markets. Keep in mind that the shorter the journey from garden to table, the better off you are nutritionally. The freshest vegetables are at farm stands or farmers' markets. In supermarkets, choose the vegetables that look liveliest. Bypass anything that is wilted, bruised, or otherwise past its prime. Another good rule of thumb for produce: the more intense the color, the more nutritionally powerful the vegetable. Go for color—dark leafy greens and yellow-orange vegetables are particularly nutritious. As Oscar Wilde, who said everything, said, "It is only shallow people who do not judge by appearance"—an insight to bear in mind when arranging food on the plate as well!

A final word on my philosophy of eating and good health: Call me old-fashioned, but to my mind common sense and moderation are the key to all things, especially when health and diet are at issue. The longer I work in the food profession, the more fads I see come and go, the more this seems to be true. The current trend in eating is low-fat, high-carbohydrate, and low-protein, a model that naturally results in lighter foods in general. Many recipes in this book are in keeping with this trend. While few of the recipes would qualify as outright diet food or even as "health" food—some contain more butter, cream, or saturated fat than current nutritional guidelines suggest—any adult who exercises regularly and eats in moderation should be able to enjoy moderate amounts of all that I have included here. I certainly do.

You might think of this book as a garden, replete with the humble and sublime flavors of the earth, conceived and laid out not in accordance with the tenets of any philosophy but simply for pleasure's sake, simply for the love of it.

Starters

Cilantro Mousse

Carrot Hummus

Wild Rice Pancakes

Grilled Stuffed Figs and Apricots

Butternut Croquettes

Cantaloupe with Black Olives

Escarole-Shallot-Apple Tarte Tatin

Goat Cheese Cake and Salad of Mixed Greens

Olive Mousse

Phyllo Strudel with Feta, Sun-Dried Tomatoes, and Olives

Tunisian Briks à la Niçoise

Grilled Vine Leaf Parcels

Baked Jerusalem Artichokes with Horseradish Crème Fraîche and Chives

Eggplant Roulades

CILANTRO MOUSSE

WINE SUGGESTIONS:
A LIGHTER-BODIED BEER
OR AN OFF-DRY WHITE WINE
SUCH AS A CALIFORNIA
GEWÜRZTRAMINER WITH A
TOUCH OF SWEETNESS

Brillant green and spicy, this is excellent served with the Thai-Inspired Seafood Salad and the Asian Sesame Noodle Salad. You must blanch the cilantro leaves if you want the mousse to be bright green; otherwise it will be greenish brown.

¼ **cup boiling water**
2 **teaspoons unflavored gelatin**
1 **large bunch of cilantro, tough stems discarded**
   Salt and freshly ground black pepper to taste
½ **cup sour cream**
½ **pound cream cheese, softened, whipped**
1 **serrano chili, seeded and finely chopped**
   Cilantro sprigs for garnish, optional

Pour the boiling water over the gelatin in a small bowl and stir until the gelatin is dissolved.

Drop the cilantro leaves into lightly salted boiling water for a minute to blanch them; drain and squeeze out all the water. Place the cilantro in a blender and add the gelatin, sour cream, cream cheese, chili, and salt and pepper. Blend until smooth. Rinse four ½-cup ramekins with cold water and pour the mixture into the dishes. Refrigerate for 1 hour or until set.

To serve, dip the bottoms of the ramekins in warm water and turn out on individual serving plates. Decorate the top of each with a perfect cilantro leaf if you wish.

CARROT HUMMUS

Pureed cooked carrots lighten this version of the flavorful Middle Eastern spread. Ready in minutes, it keeps for several days in the refrigerator. The pita bread triangles make handy scoops for the hummus, or raw cut-up vegetables can serve the purpose. The spread also makes a delicious sandwich filling.

If you have leftover cooked carrots, this is the place to use them up. Tahini (sesame seed paste) is available in most grocery stores.

2	cups cooked carrots in 1-inch pieces
1	15½-ounce can chickpeas, drained and liquid reserved
⅓	cup tahini
2	garlic cloves, peeled
⅓	cup fresh lemon juice
	Salt to taste
	Pita bread, cut into triangles, split open, and toasted

In a food processor or blender, puree the carrots, chickpeas, tahini, garlic, and lemon juice until smooth, adding reserved liquid from the chickpeas as needed to make a thick puree. Season with salt. Serve with pita triangles.

CARROT HUMMUS

•

CAULIFLOWER WITH LENTILS IN

A SPICED TOMATO SAUCE

•

RAITA WITH CUCUMBERS

AND RADISHES

•

GREEN BEANS WITH MUSTARD

SEEDS AND ALMONDS

•

COUSCOUS PUDDING WITH

PINEAPPLE AND STRAWBERRIES

WINE SUGGESTIONS:

ALSATIAN RIESLING OR AN OFF-

DRY CALIFORNIA RIESLING

Wild Rice Pancakes

Serves 6

Topped with grilled shrimp or some sautéed vegetables, these savory pancakes make an ideal first course. For lunch or a light dinner, serve them along with the Stir-Fried Asian Greens.

1   ounce pancetta or best-quality smoked bacon, cut into small pieces, optional
1   large egg, separated, at room temperature
½   cup buttermilk
3   tablespoons cornmeal
⅓   cup cooked wild rice or mixture of white and wild rice
2   tablespoons fresh corn kernels
3   tablespoons all-purpose flour
1   teaspoon baking powder
½   tablespoon minced chives or scallions
    Salt and freshly ground black pepper to taste

If you're using the pancetta, cook it in a large skillet over medium-high heat until crisp, about 3 minutes, then drain on a paper towel. Reserve 2 tablespoons of the fat.

In a small mixing bowl, beat together the egg yolk, buttermilk, and cornmeal. Let rest for 15 minutes. In a separate bowl, combine the remaining ingredients except egg white and toss to coat.

Beat the egg white until soft peaks form. Combine the cornmeal mixture with the rice mixture, then gently fold the egg white.

In the skillet, heat the reserved fat from the pancetta or 2 tablespoons vegetable oil until hot but not smoking. Using 2 tablespoons of the batter per pancake, spoon the batter into the skillet. Fry the pancakes until golden on one side, then turn them and fry until golden on the other side, about 5 minutes in all.

GRILLED STUFFED FIGS AND APRICOTS

SERVES 6

These sumptuous mouthfuls defy classification. As a rule I don't like to start a meal with something sweet, but the cheese and pancetta here convert the lush fruit into something quite savory. A lovely first course to enjoy outside, right next to the grill in the summertime.

Use the freshest fruit you can find. Late summer is the great moment for figs. See page 231 for information on fresh versus dried apricots.

6	ripe fresh figs
2 to 3	ounces Gorgonzola or other blue cheese, chilled
6	small fresh thyme sprigs
6	ounces pancetta, thinly sliced
6	ripe fresh apricots or dried apricots reconstituted in warm water for 10 minutes
2 to 3	ounces cambozola or other triple-cream soft-ripened blue cheese such as saga, blue costello, or pipo creme, chilled
6	small fresh marjoram or oregano sprigs
2	tablespoons balsamic vinegar
	Salt and freshly ground black pepper to taste
2	shallots, minced
½	cup extra-virgin olive oil
½	pound escarole or other bitter lettuce

Preheat a grill to medium-high.

Carefully cut the figs three quarters of the way through, making sure not to slice all the way through. Place about 1 heaped teaspoon of the Gorgonzola inside each fig, lay a thyme sprig over the cheese, and wrap with a piece of pancetta.

Cut the apricots in half and remove and discard the pits. Place about 1 heaped teaspoon of the cambozola cheese in the center of half of the apricot halves, lay a marjoram sprig over the cheese, place the empty halves on top, and wrap tightly with pancetta.

Chill the stuffed figs and apricots for at least 30 minutes before grilling.

GRILLED STUFFED FIGS
AND APRICOTS

•

MUSTACHE-OF-THE-DRAGON
WHEATBERRY PILAF

•

BEETS WITH RED CURRANTS

•

ROASTED PEARL ONIONS
AND SHALLOTS

•

CHOCOLATE PUDDING CAKE

WINE SUGGESTIONS:
A PROVENÇAL WHITE CASSIS
OR A LIGHT CALIFORNIA
SAUVIGNON BLANC

In a large mixing bowl, combine the vinegar, salt, and pepper. Add the shallots, then whisk in the olive oil until well blended.

Grill the figs and apricots about 6 inches from the flame for 6 to 8 minutes, turning frequently, until the pancetta is nicely brown. Cool. Add the escarole to the dressing in the bowl and toss to coat well. Serve the grilled fruit on a bed of the lightly dressed greens.

BUTTERNUT CROQUETTES

MAKES ABOUT 24 SMALL OR 12 LARGE CROQUETTES

Mellow, nutty butternut squash has flesh that is denser and creamier than pumpkin, with a color just as deep. I often make more risotto than I need just to have leftovers for these later in the week. This recipe calls for 2 cups of risotto, but you may want to make more and use the extra for the croquettes on a different occasion. They are a good hors d'oeuvre or first course and make a pleasing light main course when served on a bed of the Fresh Tomato Compote.

Risotto Croquettes

1	recipe Butternut Risotto (recipe follows)
2	large eggs, beaten
¼	pound mozzarella cheese, cut into ¼-inch cubes
¾	cup unseasoned fine bread crumbs
	Olive oil for frying
½	pound mascarpone cheese
	Small fresh sage leaves

Add the risotto to the eggs in a large mixing bowl and stir gently, taking care not to mash the rice.

Use a heaped tablespoon of the mixture to form a ball about the size of a walnut for an hors d'oeuvre or slightly larger for a first or main course. Place a cube of the mozzarella in the center and add a little more risotto if necessary to cover the cheese. Roll the ball in the bread crumbs and place on a baking sheet lined with wax paper. Shape the remaining risotto, placing the balls on the paper in a single layer. Cover with wax paper and refrigerate for 30 minutes or more.

Heat 1 inch of oil in a deep skillet until hot but not smoking. Preheat the oven to 250°F.

Fry the risotto balls, 4 or 5 at a time, for about 5 minutes, turning frequently, until golden all over. (Cooking too many balls at one time will lower the temperature of the oil and cause the balls to cook too slowly and become oily.)

Place the cooked balls in a baking dish and keep warm in the oven until

BUTTERNUT CROQUETTES

•

WINTER POT-AU-FEU WITH

PUREED EGGPLANT AND

ROASTED GARLIC

•

PARMESAN CAKE

•

SIMPLE GREEN SALAD

•

ENDIVE AND WATERCRESS

SALAD WITH

ORANGES AND FENNEL

•

ROAST APPLE CRÈME BRÛLÉE

WITH GRAVENSTEIN CAKE

WINE SUGGESTIONS:
A MEDIUM-BODIED CALIFORNIA
ZINFANDEL OR A FRENCH
BANDOL

all have been fried. They will keep in the oven only about 20 minutes at their best, so serve them as soon as possible.

Arrange the croquettes on a serving platter. Garnish each one with a spoonful of the mascarpone and a small fresh sage leaf.

Butternut Risotto

MAKES 2 CUPS

1   quart homemade or low-sodium canned chicken stock
2   tablespoons olive oil
⅓   cup minced shallot
2   cups pureed cooked butternut squash
1⅓ cups Arborio rice
1   tablespoon unsalted butter
2   tablespoons freshly grated Parmesan cheese

Bring the stock to a simmer in a saucepan and keep at a simmer while you're making the risotto.

Heat the oil in a large deep skillet, add the shallots, and sauté for 2 to 3 minutes or until translucent. Add the squash and cook for 2 to 3 minutes more. Add the rice and toss until the grains are well coated with the squash mixture. Add 1 cup of the simmering stock and cook, stirring all the time, until the liquid is absorbed. Continue to add hot stock, 1 cup at a time, allowing the rice to absorb the stock after each addition, until all the stock is used and the rice is al dente. It will take about 25 minutes altogether. Add the butter and Parmesan cheese and continue to stir until the mixture is well blended.

Eat at once as a main course or spread on a cookie sheet to cool quickly and evenly, cover, and refrigerate until you are ready to make the risotto croquettes.

CANTALOUPE WITH BLACK OLIVES

SERVES 10 TO 12

This unusual combination of sweet, perfumed fruit and bitter, salty olives comes from the Comptoir du Victuaillier restaurant (the Schmitts, proprietors) in the beautiful French hill town of Gordes in the Lubéron. For a delicious hors d'oeuvres platter, add some mild radishes, the Fennel and Asiago Twists, or some Savory Wine Biscuits.

**3   cups ripe Charentais melon or cantaloupe, preferably
       scooped out with a melon baller**
1½ cups black Niçoise olives
       Freshly ground black pepper to taste

Combine the melon and olives. Toss gently. Cover and refrigerate for at least 30 minutes so the flavors blend. Grind some fresh pepper over the top just before serving.

CANTALOUPE WITH
BLACK OLIVES

•

RISOTTO WITH
LEMON AND HERBS

•

JERUSALEM ARTICHOKE,
RADISH, AND
WATERCRESS SALAD

•

CHOCOLATE PUDDING CAKE

WINE SUGGESTIONS:
A CALIFORNIA DRY CHENIN
BLANC OR A CÔTES DU
LUBERON WHITE WINE

Charentais:
Perfumed Melons of Provence

Anyone who tastes the powerfully fragrant Charentais melons of France never forgets their unique honey-sweet flavor. The Charentais cantaloupe looks quite different from the heavily netted "cantaloupe" (actually muskmelon) of America: it is not so large and has a more rounded shape, a smaller seed cavity, and a smooth, rather delicate gray-green skin. Though named for the Charentes in the west of France, the Charentais is grown mainly in Provence around Cavaillon, where its perfume haunts the air in the summer. The flavor of this orange-red-fleshed melon is rich, complex, flowery. In Provence it is traditionally eaten as a starter course, often with salt and pepper and accompanied, as in Italy, with slices of raw ham. Alas, this lovely melon is not grown commercially here, so to eat Charentais in the United States you must raise them yourself. Most seed companies offer at least one Charentais-type melon. Burpee has one hybrid, "Honey Girl," which it believes takes especially well to American gardens (W. Atlee Burpee and Co., Warminster, PA 18974; 800-888-1447).

Escarole-Shallot-Apple Tarte Tatin

SERVES 6

This rustic tart is a savory version of the classic *tarte tatin*. It makes a good first course or light lunch served with a salad.

1½	tablespoons unsalted butter
2	teaspoons sugar
1	pound shallots, cut in half
2	green apples, peeled, cored, and thinly sliced
1	tablespoon minced fresh thyme leaves plus a few sprigs for garnish
	Salt and freshly ground black pepper to taste
1	head of escarole, about 1½ pounds, trimmed and coarsely chopped
⅓	cup homemade or low-sodium canned chicken or vegetable stock
1 or 2	teaspoons balsamic vinegar to taste
1	sheet puff pastry,* 8 to 9 ounces, thawed if frozen

Melt the butter in a 10-inch cast-iron or other ovenproof skillet; sprinkle on the sugar and remove from the heat. Arrange the shallots and apples in an alternating pattern in a single layer in the bottom of the pan with the cut side of the shallots down. Sprinkle with the thyme and season with salt and pepper.

Cook over medium-high heat for 5 minutes, reduce the heat to medium, and cook, covered, for 5 minutes more, shaking the pan gently every once in a while. Arrange the escarole over the shallot-apple mixture and gently press down. Pour in the stock and vinegar, bring to a simmer, and cook, covered, over low heat for 20 minutes or until all the liquid has cooked down and become syrupy. Remove from the heat and cool slightly.

Preheat the oven to 375°F. Roll out the puff pastry to a thickness of ⅜ inch and a diameter slightly larger than that of the skillet. Gently arrange over the pan and tuck in the excess.

Bake the tart for 30 to 35 minutes or until the pastry is golden brown and the juices are bubbling. Let cool in the pan for 5 to 10 minutes, then in-

ESCAROLE-SHALLOT-APPLE
TARTE TATIN

•

FARCI WITH FRESH WHITE
CHEESE

•

PARSLEY AND MINT SALAD

•

CARROTS WITH ANISEED

•

FRESH FRUIT WITH
GOOD SPIRITS

•

LAVENDER SHORTBREADS

WINE SUGGESTIONS:
A FRESH WHITE WINE FROM
HAUTE-SAVOIE OR AN
OREGON PINOT GRIS

vert onto a clean serving board. Garnish with thyme sprigs and cut into wedges with a pizza cutter.

*You can make from scratch puff pastry if you have the time or inclination, but this is a type of dough that freezes well, and the puff pastry sheets in the freezer section of supermarkets or gourmet stores make a more-than-acceptable substitute. Once hard to find, the frozen dough is now generally available everywhere. Try the good-quality all-butter puff pastry from Dufour Pastry Kitchens or Pepperidge Farm. Thaw the sheets according to the directions on the package and use as you would sheets of homemade dough.

Goat Cheese Cake and Salad of Mixed Greens

SERVES 6 TO 8

If you like, use herbed or peppered goat cheese for variation. The peppery punch of the watercress complements the delicate flavor of the cheese cake.

Goat Cheese Cake

Oil for the pan
1 **pound cream cheese, softened to room temperature**
10 **ounces goat cheese**
4 **large eggs**
1 **cup heavy cream**

Salad

2 **tablespoons fresh lemon juice**
5 **tablespoons extra-virgin olive oil**
Fine sea salt and freshly ground black pepper to taste
3 **cups assorted mixed greens, torn into bite-size pieces**
3 **cups watercress, large stems removed**

Preheat the oven to 350°F. Oil a 9-inch springform pan and line the bottom with parchment paper.

Cream the cheeses together until light and fluffy. Add the eggs, one at a time, beating well after each addition. Stir in the cream. Pour into the prepared pan and bake in a *bain-marie* in the preheated oven for 45 minutes to 1 hour or until the top is barely colored around the edges. Let cool for 10 minutes in the pan, then remove. This can be made several hours in advance. It should be served at room temperature or slightly chilled.

Put the lemon juice in a large salad bowl. Whisk in the oil in a thin stream until incorporated. Season with salt and pepper. Add the mixed greens and watercress and toss well.

To serve the cake and salad, give each person a slice of cake and some

SHREDDED ZUCCHINI SALAD

•

GRILLED TUNA WITH SAFFRON

VINAIGRETTE

•

GOAT CHEESE CAKE AND

SALAD OF MIXED GREENS

•

FRESH FRUIT WITH

GOOD SPIRITS

•

LAVENDER SHORTBREADS

WINE SUGGESTIONS:
A FRENCH POUILLY-FUMÉ OR A
MEDIUM-BODIED CALIFORNIA
SAUVIGNON BLANC

tossed salad on a salad plate. I like to serve this with very thin slices of walnut bread ever so lightly toasted.

The Gentle Way: Uses of the Bain-Marie

Don't be put off by the fancy name. Cooking in a *bain-marie,* or water bath, is not a tricky process and requires no particular skills or special equipment. Known to French cooks for generations, it is a simple and, above all, gentle means of cooking, reheating, keeping dishes warm, and it works on the same principle as the double boiler. Water diffuses direct heat and keeps food moist and not too hot.

The *bain-marie* itself is a shallow pan of warm or simmering water into which another dish or mold is set. The shallow pan might be a roasting pan or gratin dish or any pan that can be set directly over heat or into the oven. Foods treated this way are generally terrines, vegetable loaves, or delicate mixtures such as custards or other dishes containing eggs that require a constant, low, even heat. The silkiest *crème brûlée* comes out of a *bain-marie.*

To make a *bain-marie,* place the dish you are cooking in the shallow pan and add enough water to come about half or two thirds of the way up the sides of the dish. Bring the water to a simmer on top of the stove, transfer to a preheated oven, and bake for the time specified in the recipe. The water should never boil.

A *bain-marie* is also useful for heating or keeping dishes warm. To reheat, place the dish in the water bath, bring the water to a simmer on top of the stove, and heat to the desired temperature in the oven. To keep a finished dish warm, set the mold or dish in a hot but not simmering water bath. Check the level of the water; to ensure thorough heating, it should be well up the sides of the dish.

OLIVE MOUSSE

MAKES EIGHT ½-CUP SERVINGS

This is a great first course, very simple if you have an excellent jar of tapenade on hand in the pantry. Provide guests with thinly sliced, lightly toasted French bread or crackers on which to spread the unmolded mousse.

½   **cup boiling water**
2   **tablespoons unflavored gelatin**
1½ **cups heavy cream**
2   **cups tapenade, homemade or store-bought**
1   **tablespoon finely chopped basil**
    Salt and freshly ground black pepper to taste
3   **small black imported olives for garnish**
2   **tablespoons balsamic vinegar**
2   **shallots, minced**
½   **cup extra-virgin olive oil**
½   **pound *mesclun* (any combination of small, young lettuces or greens)**

Pour the boiling water over the gelatin in a small bowl and stir until the gelatin is dissolved.

In a medium bowl, beat the cream until stiff peaks form. Fold in some of the beaten cream into the cooled gelatin, then fold the gelatin back into the cream. Now fold in the tapenade and basil. Season with salt and pepper.

Gently pour the mixture into 8 individual ½-cup molds. Refrigerate for at least 2 hours, preferably overnight.

To serve, dip the bottom of the molds very quickly in hot water and invert onto individual serving plates. Pit the olives, halve them lengthwise, and decorate the top of each mousse with half an olive.

In a large mixing bowl, combine the vinegar with salt and pepper to taste. Add the shallots, then whisk in the olive oil until well blended. Add the *mesclun* and toss to coat well. Surround each mousse with a little of the salad mixture and serve.

OLIVE MOUSSE

•

SAVORY WINE BISCUITS

•

VEGETABLE RISOTTO WITH
CARROT, CELERY, AND
PARSLEY BROTH

•

PEACH AND
BLUEBERRY BUCKLE

WINE SUGGESTIONS:
A CHIANTI CLASSICO RISERVA
OR A CALIFORNIA SANGIOVESE

ALBUQUERQUE ACADEMY
LIBRARY

Phyllo Strudel with Feta, Sun-Dried Tomatoes, and Olives

MAKES 10 PIECES

This pretty and easy appetizer is delicious with drinks or with a simple salad course.

3   sheets frozen phyllo dough, thawed according to package directions
1   tablespoon oil from olives or sun-dried tomatoes
1   cup cubed feta cheese
¾   cup pitted and chopped imported olives, green or black or both
1   tablespoon minced drained oil-packed sun-dried tomato
    Freshly ground black pepper to taste
    Butter for the baking sheet

Preheat the oven to 400°F.

Unfold the pastry sheets carefully. Place on a damp cloth. Using a pastry brush, brush each sheet lightly with oil. Place the sheets directly over each other.

To make the filling, in a mixing bowl combine the feta cheese, olives, and sun-dried tomato; season with 2 or 3 grinds of pepper.

Place the filling in a single strip along the edge of the dough closest to you. Roll like a jelly roll. Place the strudel on a lightly buttered baking sheet and brush with a little more oil. (The strudel may be wrapped in plastic and then in foil at this stage and frozen for several weeks or refrigerated until ready to bake uncut. Chilling the strudel before baking makes it easier to slice later.)

Mark individual servings of the strudel with a sharp knife and cut on the diagonal into 10 pieces; bake for about 35 minutes or until golden brown. Cool for about 5 minutes before serving.

ALBUQUERQUE ACADEMY
LIBRARY

Tunisian Briks à la Niçoise

SERVES 2

A marvelous hybrid. Tunisian cooks have probably never heard of the traditional *Niçoise,* and cooks across the Mediterranean in the south of France would be startled to see their salad classic with crispy filled pastry placed front and center. Paula Wolfert's authoritative recipe for briks in her revised *Mediterranean Cooking* (1995) was my jumping-off point for this recipe.

The brik is Tunisia's answer to China's spring roll, a snack eaten any time of day consisting of a paper-thin sheet of dough filled with any of hundreds of savory stuffings and then quick-fried. The Tunisians use a special pastry of semolina and water called *malsouqua,* but our handy frozen supermarket phyllo performs well as a stand-in.

Although you can double or triple the recipe, this is a tricky dish to do for more than 2 or 3; only one brik should be fried at a time, and the pastry-wrapped eggs will cook past perfection if reheated.

1   recipe Lemon-Anchovy Dressing see page 174, capers omitted
2   tablespoons finely minced onion
1   tablespoon minced parsley
1   teaspoon olive oil
½   teaspoon drained capers
1   3½-ounce can Genova or other Italian oil-packed tuna,* drained
4   sheets of frozen phyllo dough, thawed according to package directions
2   tablespoons melted butter
2   medium eggs
     Salt and freshly ground black pepper to taste
     Vegetable oil for frying
3   cups mixed lettuces
6   small red-skinned potatoes, cooked and quartered
½   pound green beans, cooked al dente
1   vine-ripened tomato, quartered
     Lemon quarters for garnish

ROAST CORN AND

CHILI GAZPACHO

•

TUNISIAN BRIKS À LA NIÇOISE

•

STRAWBERRIES IN LEMON

VERBENA WITH FRESH CHEESE

ICE CREAM

WINE SUGGESTIONS:

A CRISP OREGON PINOT GRIS

OR A SPANISH VINO VERDE

In a large bowl, whisk together the ingredients for the dressing and set aside.

In a small sauté pan over medium-high heat, cook the onion and parsley in the oil until soft but not brown, about 3 minutes. Add the capers and tuna and cook, stirring, for a minute or two.

To make the briks, brush the sheets of phyllo with the melted butter, placing one on top of another according to the package directions. Cut the layered sheets in half to form two 7- by 9-inch rectangles. Place half the tuna mixture on each dough rectangle about 2 inches from one of the corners, break an egg over the filling, season with salt and pepper, and fold the top over the filling. Then, beginning at the filling end, fold up into triangles like a flag, beginning at the filling end. Seal the edges by folding them onto themselves and pressing together.

In a deep saucepan, heat about 3 inches of oil until it is hot but not smoking. Gently slide one of the briks into the oil and fry until puffy and brown, about 1 minute. (Do not overcook; when served, the egg should be just soft-cooked.) Transfer to paper towels to drain and repeat the process with the second brik.

Toss the lettuces in the dressing until coated evenly, then divide between 2 serving plates. Place one brik on each serving and surround with the potatoes, green beans, and tomatoes. Garnish with lemon for squeezing over the crispy pastry.

*Genova tuna in little gold cans from Italy costs more than standard brands of tuna but tastes about five times better. In fact, packed in good-quality olive oil, it actually tastes like tuna. Look for it in well-stocked supermarkets or Italian groceries.

Grilled Vine Leaf Parcels

Stuffed grape leaves are doubly delicious when seared by a quick grilling. The bite-size wrap-ups can be made ahead, even held for several days in the refrigerator, and grilled at the last minute. Serve them as an appetizer or alongside a salad.

2	cups cooked basmati rice
½	cup ricotta cheese
1	cup crumbled feta cheese
2	tablespoons plain yogurt
	Finely grated zest and juice of 1 lemon
½	cup finely chopped sun-dried tomatoes
¼	cup pine nuts, toasted
¼	cup finely chopped shallot
	Salt and freshly ground black pepper to taste
1	10-ounce jar vine leaves, rinsed, drained, and patted dry
	Olive oil

In a bowl, mix together the rice, ricotta, feta, yogurt, lemon zest, tomatoes, pine nuts, and shallot; add salt and pepper.

Place one of the vine leaves on a work surface. Put 1 heaped teaspoon of the filling in the center of the leaf. Fold over the stalk end to cover the mixture, then fold in the sides and continue rolling up the leaf to form a small parcel. Repeat with the remaining leaves.

Preheat a grill to medium-hot. Brush the vine leaf parcels all over with olive oil and grill 6 inches from the heat, turning once, until lightly charred on both sides, about 3 minutes. Drizzle with the lemon juice and a little olive oil and serve.

Grilled Vine Leaf Parcels

•

Eggplant Torte with Fresh Tomato Compote

•

Savory Baked Ricotta

•

Zucchini Cake with Fruit and Nuts

Wine suggestions: a simple Coteaux du Languedoc or a lighter-bodied California Cabernet Sauvignon

Baked Jerusalem Artichokes with Horseradish Crème Fraîche and Chives

SERVES 8

Slow-roasting the Jerusalem artichokes turns them a delicious golden brown, while caramelizing the natural sugars gives them a great flavor boost. Topped with a little horseradish cream and chives, they're the perfect mouthful with a glass of your favorite champagne.

1   pound Jerusalem artichokes, well scrubbed but not peeled
2   tablespoons olive oil
    Juice of 1 lemon
    Salt and freshly ground black pepper to taste
4   bay leaves
2   cups crème fraîche or sour cream
2   tablespoons freshly grated horseradish or drained bottled horseradish
2   tablespoons chopped fresh chives

Preheat the oven to 400°F.

Place the artichokes close together in one layer in a heavy roasting pan. Coat with olive oil, squeeze on the lemon juice, season with salt and pepper, and tuck in the bay leaves. Cover with foil and cook for 20 to 25 minutes or until cooked through and golden. Remove to a rack set over a pan to catch the drippings and let cool. Remove the bay leaves.

Combine the crème fraîche and horseradish in a small bowl. To serve, place a spoonful of the horseradish cream on top of each artichoke and sprinkle with some chopped chives.

Eggplant Roulades

I learned this recipe from Karen Mitchell, owner of the wonderful Model Bakery in St. Helena. Grilling the eggplant slices adds a delicious smoky flavor. Fresh sheep's milk ricotta is the secret ingredient; look for it in specialty cheese shops or Italian markets. These little bundles make a marvelous first course, served alone or with a simple salad, but are also an excellent accompaniment to a risotto main course.

3	pounds small Italian or Japanese eggplant, cap and stem ends removed, sliced no thicker than ⅛ inch
½	cup olive oil plus oil for brushing eggplant
	Salt and freshly ground black pepper to taste
2	cups fresh ricotta, preferably made from fresh sheep's milk
2	tablespoons minced fresh mint
3	tablespoons minced fresh basil
2	tablespoons minced fresh chives
⅓	cup balsamic vinegar
	Additional herbs for garnish, optional

Preheat a grill or broiler. Brush both sides of the eggplant slices with olive oil and season with salt and pepper. In a bowl, combine the ricotta and herbs.

Grill the eggplant slices over medium-hot coals, turning, until the flesh is soft and slightly charred, about 6 minutes. Drain on a brown paper bag to remove excess oil.

Using a knife, spread some of the cheese mixture over the eggplant in a thin layer. Roll the eggplant over the filling like a jelly roll and place, seam side down, on a deep serving plate. Then drizzle on the vinegar and ½ cup oil and decorate with additional herbs if you wish. Serve at room temperature.

CANTALOUPE WITH

BLACK OLIVES

•

EGGPLANT ROULADES

•

RISOTTO WITH

LEMON AND HERBS

•

JERUSALEM ARTICHOKE,

RADISH, AND

WATERCRESS SALAD

•

CHOCOLATE PUDDING CAKE

WINE SUGGESTIONS:
A CALIFORNIA DRY CHENIN
BLANC OR A CÔTES DU
LUBERON WHITE WINE

Soups and Stocks

STOCKS: Vegetable and Dried Mushroom Consommé

Golden Veal Stock

Ginger Broth

Chicken Stock

Simple Vegetable Stock

SOUPS: Green Lentil and Escarole Soup

Pumpkin Ravioli in Ginger Broth with Curry Oil

Tierra Farms Black Bean Chili

Carrot-Rhubarb Soup with Cinnamon Croutons

Minted Snow Pea and Potato Soup

Winter Pot-au-Feu with Pureed Eggplant and Roasted Garlic

Roast Corn and Chili Gazpacho

Minestrone with Rosemary-Chili Pesto

Mexican Hot and Sour Soup with Hominy

Springwater Mushroom Broth

White Beans and Fennel au Pistou

Borscht with Cabbage and Apples

Bouillabaisse of Fennel and Potato

Tangy Greens and Wheatberry Soup

Double Celery Soup with Apple and Dill

Cold Cucumber Soup with Dill

On Stocks and Stock Making

There's hardly a soup, sauce, or stew that doesn't benefit from a rich, long-simmered stock, and this book is full of recipes that call for the genuine homemade article. Stocks, or broths, are not hard to make, but they do in most cases require the luxury of time. What they give back in depth of flavor is well worth your commitment.

Serve a nourishing stock just as it is or use it as a base for soups or reduce it to make a sauce. Stocks are almost endlessly useful; they can be cooked again with a handful of fresh herbs and chopped vegetables, work as the bouillon for poaching fish or chicken, form the rounded background for a risotto or pot-au-feu. Vegetable-based stocks are both easier to make and more delicate and should be used as soon as possible. The full-bodied meat stocks provide a pure meat essence that is, to the nearly vegetarian palate, just as satisfying as a serving of beef or chicken.

You will notice that these recipes do not call for salt. Resisting the urge to salt at the outset allows for flexibility. If you intend to reduce a salted stock, the concentrated result will be too salty. You can always season the finished sauce or dish to taste.

STOCKS

VEGETABLE AND DRIED MUSHROOM CONSOMMÉ

Chef Hubert Keller of the brilliant Fleur de Lys in San Francisco kindly shared this gem of a recipe. The mushrooms give the easy stock a lush flavor and a lovely golden color not unlike that of beef consommé. For cooking stocks and stews, Hubert suggests buying the lesser grade of dried mushrooms. The little pieces impart the same flavor and are strained out at the end.

You can use almost any herb in this recipe except rosemary, which will overpower the stock. The fresher this stock is, the better.

2   medium leeks, both green and white parts, split in half
           lengthwise, well rinsed, and diced
½   small celery root, peeled and diced, or 3 outer celery
           ribs, diced
4   shallots, coarsely chopped
1   large tomato, seeded
3   medium carrots, diced
10   fresh or dried mushrooms, diced
3   garlic cloves, coarsely chopped
3   parsley sprigs
8 to 10 fresh basil leaves
1   fresh thyme sprig
2   bay leaves
2   fresh chervil sprigs
2   fresh cilantro or tarragon sprigs, optional
10   cups cold water, preferably springwater

In a large saucepan, combine all the ingredients. Bring slowly to a boil, then reduce to a simmer. Simmer for 20 minutes, turn off the heat, cover, and let rest for 20 minutes. Strain through a strainer lined with several layers of rinsed cheesecloth. Discard the solids and store the consommé, covered, in the refrigerator for up to 3 days.

GOLDEN VEAL STOCK

If you make just one stock in this book, make this one. Veal stock is compatible with vegetable dishes that call for chicken stock, but it imparts a depth of flavor no canned stock can offer. If you're trying to cut down on your meat consumption or simply looking for a way to flavor a dish without adding fat to it, veal stock works a neat trick, supplying just enough meat essence to satisfy the taste for a serving of meat.

My friend Madeleine Kamman stresses the importance of this stock in her excellent books (the 1971 classic *The Making of a Cook* is my favorite) and to her students—and Madeleine is the best teacher in the food world today. Veal stock has a unique flavor that is less tart and heavy than that of beef or lamb stock, and it can be reduced to a few golden tablespoons of syrupy demi-glace without becoming gummy. It is the preferred base for all reduction sauces.

Some recipes call for roasting only bones, but a veal stock made only from bones will have a chalky taste. You do need a little meat.

Once this stock is strained and cooled, I like to pack it in pint containers so that I can take what I need from refrigerator or freezer to use full-strength as a base for cooking vegetables or grains or to reduce in half for sauce making.

1	**veal breast, unboned, about 5 pounds**
2	**pounds veal bones**
6	**quarts water, preferably springwater**
4	**carrots, coarsely chopped**
2	**onions, quartered**
1	**leek, split in half lengthwise, well rinsed, and coarsely chopped**

Preheat the oven to 400°F.

Put the veal breast and bones in a large roasting pan and brown in the oven for about 40 minutes, turning once or twice, until the meat and bones are golden and the meat releases some of its juices.

Pour off the fat and set aside the meat and bones while you deglaze the pan with water. Place the roasting pan on the stove over high heat. Add 1 cup of the water and stir with a wooden spoon until almost all the liquid has evaporated and the meat juices and bits at the bottom of the pan begin to caramelize. Repeat the process twice more, adding another cup of water each time.

Scrape the caramelized meat juices and bits into a slow cooker and cover with the remaining water. Bring to a simmer, add the vegetables, and simmer, partially covered, on the medium setting for 24 hours.

Cool for 10 minutes. Strain through a strainer lined with several layers of rinsed cheesecloth. Discard the solids and cool to room temperature. Refrigerate until the fat has solidified on the surface. Discard the fat and divide the stock among pint containers. Store in the refrigerator for up to 1 week or freeze for up to 3 months.

Ginger Broth

This is the light, fragrant stock used in the Pumpkin Ravioli in Ginger Broth with Curry Oil. It's delicious as a bouillon for poaching fish or shellfish or as the base for any Asian-style soup.

- 1 **large onion, quartered**
- 3 **large carrots, coarsely chopped**
- 2 **plum tomatoes, quartered**
- **6 to 7 thin slices fresh ginger**
- **3 to 4 fresh cilantro sprigs, optional**
- 1 **teaspoon black peppercorns**
- 2 **quarts homemade or low-sodium canned chicken stock or water**
- 1½ **cups dry white wine**

In a large nonaluminum stockpot, combine the first 6 ingredients with the stock and wine. Bring to a boil, then reduce the heat and simmer, uncovered, for 20 minutes. Let rest for 20 minutes, then strain through a strainer lined with several layers of rinsed cheesecloth and discard all solids. The broth can be used immediately or cooled and refrigerated for up to 2 days or frozen for up to 3 months.

CHICKEN STOCK

This full-bodied all-purpose stock takes some time to make. If you haven't the patience, a good-quality canned chicken broth makes an okay substitute if it's low-fat, low-sodium, and not destined for a reduction.

1   fresh 4- to 5-pound chicken, preferably a stewing hen, cut into 8 pieces, plus the giblets
6   quarts cool water, preferably springwater
6   carrots, diced
3   onions, diced
6   leeks, white part only, split in half lengthwise, well rinsed, and cut into ¼-inch dice
    Bouquet garni: 8 parsley sprigs, 6 fresh thyme sprigs, 1 fresh tarragon sprig, and 2 bay leaves wrapped in cheesecloth and tied with string
8   peppercorns

Rinse the chicken pieces under cool water several times. Place them with the giblets in a large stockpot. Cover with the water and bring to a boil, skimming off and discarding the scum. Add the vegetables and bouquet garni, bring to a second boil, and skim again. Reduce the heat to very low and simmer, partially covered, for 6 to 8 hours, adding the peppercorns during the last hour of cooking. Remove from the heat and let rest for 10 minutes.

Strain the stock through a strainer lined with several layers of rinsed cheesecloth. Discard the solids and let the stock cool to room temperature. Refrigerate for at least 6 hours, then skim off the hardened fat from the surface. Use within 3 days or freeze for up to 3 months.

Once thawed, return the stock to a boil and skim again before using.

Simple Vegetable Stock

The secret agent that brings together the elements in so many vegetable dishes, basic vegetable stock is much simpler to make than a stock of veal or chicken—and a lot more perishable. This one holds for little more than a day. You can add or substitute other fresh vegetables or herbs to the recipe, but make sure they complement the dish you're preparing. This stock is also great by itself as a pick-me-up any time of day.

- 2 **carrots, sliced**
- 2 **onions, sliced**
- 4 **leeks, white part only, split in half lengthwise, well rinsed, and chopped**
- 2 **celery ribs, chopped**
- 2 **tablespoons unsalted butter**
- 10 **cups cool water, preferably springwater**
   Bouquet garni: 8 parsley sprigs, 2 bay leaves, and several fresh sprigs of other herbs such as savory, chervil, basil, or tarragon, wrapped in cheesecloth and tied with string

In a stockpot over medium-high heat, sauté the vegetables in the butter until soft but not brown, about 4 minutes. Add the water and bring to a boil. Add the bouquet garni and simmer, uncovered, for 2 hours. Remove from the heat and let rest for 10 minutes. Strain through a strainer lined with several layers of rinsed cheesecloth. Discard the solids and cool the stock to room temperature. Store, covered, in the refrigerator. Use within 24 hours. This stock does not freeze well.

SOUPS

GREEN LENTIL AND ESCAROLE SOUP

SERVES 6

France's small, naturally spicy green lentils—*lentilles de Puy*—may be the most expensive lentils on earth, but their superior flavor takes this peasant-style dish straight uptown. A cross between a soup and a stew, it owes its inspiration to a Lebanese dish traditionally served with turnip pickles. Choose your own favorite pickle to accompany it.

2	tablespoons unsalted butter
2	medium yellow onions, finely chopped
2	garlic cloves, minced
1	medium carrot, diced
1	cup French green lentils, washed and picked over*
1	bay leaf
3	canned whole tomatoes, drained, seeded, and coarsely chopped
2	quarts water or homemade or low-sodium canned chicken stock
½	large head of escarole, sliced crosswise into 1-inch strips, or 6 cups Swiss chard or spinach leaves
½	pound extra-wide egg noodles
	Salt and freshly ground black pepper to taste
	Fresh lemon juice to taste

In a large heavy stockpot, melt the butter over medium heat. Add the onions, garlic, and carrot and sauté until tender, about 10 minutes, stirring frequently to brown evenly. Add the lentils, bay leaf, tomatoes, and water. Bring to a simmer and cook, uncovered, until the lentils are tender, about 40 minutes. Add the escarole and cook for 5 minutes more. Bring the soup to a boil, add the noodles, and cook until done, about 4 minutes; do not overcook. Adjust the seasoning with salt, pepper, and lemon juice.

*Seek out the strikingly mottled slate-green *lentilles de Puy* from the Auvergne.

GREEN LENTIL AND

ESCAROLE SOUP

•

SEAWEED FOUGASSE

•

AVOCADO-PAPAYA SALAD

•

BLACK SESAME TUILES

WITH ICE CREAM

WINE SUGGESTIONS:

A DRIER CALIFORNIA ROSÉ OR

TAVEL ROSE

They have a distinctly peppery flavor and hold their shape when cooked. Specialty food stores carry them, or you can mail-order them from Dean & Deluca, 560 Broadway, New York, NY 10012; 212-431-1691. For this dish you can substitute brown, purple, or sweet midget lentils, but the large green domestic lentils so popular in Middle Eastern cooking are really too mild.

PUMPKIN RAVIOLI IN GINGER BROTH WITH CURRY OIL

SERVES 6

This East-meets-West dish relies on Asian flavorings for its zip. For the dumplings I use wonton wrappers bought at the supermarket instead of the more conventional fresh pasta dough—an appropriate adaptation and a real time-saver.

The ravioli can be made several days ahead, wrapped well in plastic wrap, and refrigerated. Take them directly from the refrigerator to poach them so the wrappers don't get sticky.

½	cup (¼ pound uncooked, trimmed pumpkin) pumpkin puree (not pie filling) or other cooked and pureed winter squash
1	tablespoon unsalted butter, cut into small pieces, at room temperature
1	large egg yolk
½	cup grated Asiago cheese
½	teaspoon Chinese five-spice powder
¼	teaspoon salt
1	10-ounce package 3-inch-square wonton wrappers, the thinnest you can find

Curry Oil

½	cup vegetable oil, such as canola, corn, or peanut oil
1	tablespoon curry powder
1	recipe Ginger Broth (page 32)
¼	cup thinly sliced scallion greens for garnish
	Cilantro leaves for garnish

In a large bowl, combine the pumpkin, butter, egg yolk, cheese, spice powder, and salt. Mix well. The puree should be firm and hold together; if it is too soft, add a little more cheese.

PUMPKIN RAVIOLI IN GINGER BROTH WITH CURRY OIL

•

WILD MUSHROOM BREAD PUDDING

•

CARROTS WITH CRANBERRIES AND DILL

•

LEAVES OF BRUSSELS SPROUTS WITH CHESTNUTS

•

DRIED FRUIT WITH GOOD SPIRITS

•

SOUTHERN PERSIMMON BREAD WITH CORN AND BLACK WALNUTS

WINE SUGGESTIONS: A YOUNG RED CÔTES-DU-RHÔNE OR A CALIFORNIA ZINFANDEL. IF YOU ARE SERVING THIS AROUND THANKSGIVING, TRY A NEWLY RELEASED BEAUJOLAIS NOUVEAU.

To shape the wontons, arrange half the wrappers on a lightly floured surface. Mound a heaped teaspoonful of the filling in the center of one square of dough. Moisten the edges with a bit of water and place another wonton wrapper on top. Cut the edges of the ravioli with a fluted-edged pasta wheel to trim and seal them.

Repeat with the rest of the wonton wrappers. If you're not going to cook them immediately, arrange them in a single layer on a cookie sheet lined with wax or parchment paper, cover with plastic wrap, and refrigerate.

Combine the oil and curry in a small bowl and let rest for at least 30 minutes. Use only the oil at the top of the mixture or strain through 2 layers of rinsed cheesecloth.

To cook the ravioli, bring the broth to a simmer in a large stockpot. Slide the wontons into the pot, stir gently, and allow the stock to return to a simmer. Cook the ravioli until they float to the surface, about 5 minutes. Be careful not to overcook them, or the filling will ooze out.

Under Wraps:
The Handy Wonton

Wonton skins make quick and easy work of wrapping up any number of savory fillings. Just because they're readily available in supermarkets and Asian groceries, there's no reason to consider store-bought wrappers inferior to homemade; in fact, they're easier to work with, and they won't cook up mushy or chewy. Commercial wontons leave you free to improvise with fillings and sauces, and they keep well—park them in the refrigerator for a week or freeze them for up to two months.

Are wonton skins really pasta? Yes, they're just flour, eggs, and salt. They take well to boiling and steaming as well as deep- and panfrying. By themselves wontons are bland, but this quality works to advantage when they're combined with bravely spiced fillings and piquant dipping sauces.

Buy the 3-inch squares for ravioli or other dumpling pillows or, for pot stickers, choose the round gyoza wrappers (pot sticker skins). Look for a count of about 50 wrappers to a 10-ounce package—any fewer and the dumplings will taste unpleasantly doughy when cooked.

Tierra Farms Black Bean Chili

Wine suggestions: Beer, preferably an amber beer served with wedges of lime, would be best with this menu. Or try a young Zinfandel or Australian Shiraz.

This is by far the best all-vegetable chili I have ever tasted. Lee and Wayne James raise a wide variety of chilies at their Tierra Farms ranch in northern California, and this is their recipe. Chipotles, a key component, are smoke-dried jalapeño peppers. They are packed with rich heat and haunting smokiness; when you add them to a vegetarian dish, they bring a complexity of flavor that makes it seem as if you've added about 20 other ingredients. Adding vinegar is a Cuban trick that brings out the natural sweetness of the beans.

2 cups dried black beans, picked over for stones
2 tablespoons olive oil
2 cups diced onion
1 tablespoon minced garlic
1 tomato, diced
2 bay leaves
2 tablespoons crushed cumin seeds
1 teaspoon ground red chili or cayenne
1 quart water
1 to 2 whole "tam" jalapeño chipotles* or 1 Mexican chipotle or 1 to 2 tablespoons chopped canned chipotles *en adobo*
3 tablespoons white vinegar
1 tablespoon light brown sugar
2 teaspoons salt

Place the beans in a large pot with enough cold water to cover. Soak for 4–6 hours or overnight. Drain and discard the soaking liquid.

Heat the oil in a skillet over medium heat; add the onion and sauté until translucent, about 3 minutes. Stir in the garlic and tomato. Sauté for 3 minutes, then add the bay leaves, cumin seeds, and ground chili. Stir well.

Place the beans in a heavy pot and add about 1 quart fresh water. Stir in the onion-tomato mixture. Add the chipotles (add 1 for mildly spicy-smoky flavor, 2 if you want the beans really spicy). Stir in the vinegar and brown sugar. Simmer the beans over low heat for 1 hour or until tender to the bite but not mushy. Add the salt during the last minutes of cooking.

Note: To reconstitute freshly dried peppers, plump them in very hot water until soft and pliable, about 10 or 20 minutes; imported chilies, often drier to start with, may need as much as an hour's soaking. Do not over-soak. What you want is a softened, pliable chili, the flesh partially reconstituted but not mushy. Remove the seeds and veins before using.

Idea: Try a sauce of pureed chipotles, Asiago cheese, garlic, lime, and chopped cilantro on summer's fresh corn on the cob.

*The "tam" jalapeño is a mild form of the pepper recently developed in Texas. If you can't get the "tam" chipotle, use the chipotles from Mexico, either dried or canned in sauce (chipotle *en adobo*), available in ethnic markets or the specialty foods section of your supermarket, if you're lucky. Or order your fresh smoked chipotles, pure and unadulterated, direct from Tierra Farms at 707-433-5666.

CARROT-RHUBARB SOUP
WITH CINNAMON CROUTONS

SERVES 6

CARROT-RHUBARB SOUP WITH

CINNAMON CROUTONS

•

ROASTED BARLEY AND WILD

MUSHROOM PILAF

•

CHIFFONADE OF RADICCHIO

WITH BAKED GOAT CHEESE

•

MAPLE PEARS WITH

CARDAMOM CREAM

WINE SUGGESTIONS:

A SPANISH RIOJA OR A

MEDIUM-BODIED

CALIFORNIA NEBBIOLO

There never seem to be enough ways to use tart, field-grown rhubarb when it makes its brief appearance in the spring. This unusual combination keeps everyone guessing on the ingredients.

2	shallots, minced
2	tablespoons unsalted butter
1½	pounds carrots, cut into ½-inch pieces
½	pound rhubarb, cut into ½-inch lengths
½	cup frozen orange juice concentrate
1½	cups chicken or vegetable stock, preferably homemade
2	cups half-and-half, milk, or low-fat milk
	Salt and freshly ground black pepper to taste
6	½-inch-thick slices sourdough bread
	Olive oil
1	garlic clove, peeled
1	teaspoon cinnamon, freshly grated if possible
	Fresh chervil sprigs for garnish

In a large saucepan over medium heat, sauté the shallots in the butter until soft but not browned, about 3 minutes. Add the carrots and cook, stirring to prevent sticking, over medium-high heat for 10 to 12 minutes or until the carrots are just tender. Add the rhubarb and orange juice, cover, and cook for 4 to 5 minutes more.

In a blender, puree the carrot and rhubarb mixture with the stock in several batches until smooth. Return to a clean saucepan and combine with the half-and-half. Add salt and pepper and heat thoroughly before serving.

Preheat the oven to 350°F. Brush the bread on both sides with some of the olive oil. Arrange on a baking sheet in a single layer. Toast the bread until nicely browned on both sides in the oven. Rub the bread on one side with the garlic clove and dust with cinnamon.

To serve, put one slice of the bread in each warm bowl and ladle the hot soup over it. Serve immediately garnished with a chervil sprig.

Note: To conserve all of rhubarb's bright flavor, cook this highly acidic vegetable in nonreactive pans such as stainless steel, enameled cast iron, or anodized aluminum.

Minted Snow Pea and Potato Soup

Those of us who garden, no matter how organized we try to be, are always faced with the "vegetable that got away." In spring it's the peas. Seeded in cool weather, they slowly twine their way up the supports we have given them, and then, presto, seemingly overnight we are the proud owner of a vast vertical pea plantation. Many of the little pods manage to elude even the most tenacious picker, who in the end is left with bushels of not-so-tender peas.

This light, fresh-tasting soup uses up a bumper crop of slightly over-the-hill snow peas. Of course, it's equally good, maybe better, made with new, tender young snow peas.

1½	tablespoons olive oil
¼	cup sliced shallot
1	pound waxy potatoes, peeled and cut into 1-inch pieces, about 2½ cups
1	quart chicken or vegetable stock, preferably homemade
1	pound snow peas, trimmed and cut in half
1	cup tightly packed fresh mint leaves, coarsely chopped
	Salt and freshly ground black pepper to taste
½	cup sour cream, crème fraîche, or plain yogurt
	tender pea shoots for garnish

In a large saucepan, heat the olive oil over medium-high heat, add the shallots, and sauté for 3 to 4 minutes or until wilted but not browned. Add the potatoes and stock, bring to a simmer, and cook, uncovered, for 15 to 20 minutes or until the potatoes are very tender. Add the snow peas and simmer for 3 to 4 minutes more. Stir in the mint leaves.

Remove the mixture from the heat and allow to cool for 10 minutes. Puree in small batches in a blender until smooth. (You can use a food processor, but you'll lose the bright green color.)

Return the soup to the saucepan, which has been wiped clean, and heat through. Season with salt and pepper.

Garnish each serving with a tablespoon of sour cream and top with tender pea shoots if you have them.

Food Processor vs. Blender:
Which Machine for Which Job?

If one day you decided to invest in a food processor, I hope you did not throw out your blender in a fit of overconfidence in the abilities of the new machine. True, the processor is a marvelous kitchen aid. Amazingly versatile, it can grind, grate, mince, and blend. It can chop meat, knead dough, mix cake and cookie batter, whip egg whites, process fruits, slice whole vegetables, cut french fries, and much, much more. It's unbeatable for making rough-textured pastes and sauces such as tapenade. But you need a blender, too.

A blender is superior to the processor in pureeing, in liquefying soft foods, making smooth soups, and whipping up in seconds the frothiest of liquid refreshments. (My children passionately love a blender mixture of fresh strawberries and orange juice.) While providing foods with the smoothest possible texture, it also has the edge in preserving color, an important advantage when you're working with the highly vibrant hues of beets or basil (pesto) or peas (soup). It's the quickness of the action produced by its powerful motor that seems to perform this trick. (The motor of the food processor is more powerful than that of some blenders, but the power and punch of a top-quality, heavy-duty blender meets or exceeds that of the standard processor.)

Be careful when using a blender. Make sure it's shut off when you finish working with it. Be careful blending hot foods; the top can fly off—a real hazard. Try cooling the foods somewhat before you blend them or put a layer of plastic wrap over the top of the glass container before closing with the lid. A blender performs best if you pulse the motor, using a regular on-off rhythm with the setting button you have chosen. Always buy the best piece of equipment you can afford. If you can, buy a top-of-the-line variable-speed Oster blender. It's a thing of beauty, very sturdy, performing a variety of functions reliably and well.

The food processor is trumped, too, in the execution of certain special tasks by two other devices. Equip yourself with a stainless-steel or wooden mandoline. This traditional—and expensive—hand-driven tool does a better job than the processor at extra-thin slicing of hard vegetables such as potatoes, cabbage, and beets and at julienne and waffle cutting. The mini food processor is a machine I love for another chore: mincing garlic and herbs, grinding nuts, and grating a few ounces of cheese. But I have set mine aside for a special purpose: it does a terrific job grinding toasted spices, indispensable in the preparation of fresh Mexican, Middle Eastern, or Indian spice blends.

To help you fit the tool to the task, here are some specialties of the blender and the food processor:

BLENDER	**FOOD PROCESSOR**
FINE-TEXTURED SAUCES	ROUGH-TEXTURED SAUCES
PESTO	TAPENADE
THIN MIXTURES	THICK MIXTURES
PUREEING COOKED VEGETABLES	CHOPPING, SLICING, SHREDDING, AND
LIQUEFYING SOFT FRUITS AND	GRATING RAW VEGETABLES
VEGETABLES	CHOPPING HERBS
SMOOTH SOUPS	JULIENNE CUTTING
FROTHY DRINKS	BREAD DOUGH
	SHORT-CRUST PASTRY
	COOKIE DOUGH
	CUTTING FRENCH FRIES
	MAYONNAISE

Winter Pot-au-Feu with Pureed Eggplant and Roasted Garlic

SERVES 6

Nourishing, soul-satisfying pot-au-feu is a simmer-on-the-back-of-the-stove classic of French cooking. This garden-variety version is every bit as hearty and sustaining as the meat-intensive original, with a shorter cooking time.

The eggplant and garlic purees can be made up to a day in advance; bring them to room temperature before serving.

1	small eggplant
	Olive oil
1	head of garlic
	Salt and freshly ground black pepper to taste
2	quarts veal, chicken, or vegetable stock, preferably homemade
1½	cups peeled and julienned sweet potatoes
2	cups tiny potatoes, unpeeled
1	cup peeled and thinly sliced parsnip
1	cup well-rinsed and thinly sliced leek, white and light green parts only
1	cup peeled rutabaga in 1-inch chunks
1	cup thinly sliced carrot
1½	cups green beans in ½-inch diagonal pieces
1	cup sliced zucchini, cut into ½-inch rounds
2	cups coarsely chopped Swiss chard, tough veins removed
	Grated zest of 1 lemon
¼	cup minced parsley

Preheat the oven to 375°F.

Poke several holes in the eggplant. Pour a little oil onto a baking sheet. Roll the eggplant in the oil and bake until soft, about 1 hour. Set aside until cool to the touch.

Cut the top off the garlic head and discard. Pour a little oil over the head and lightly salt and pepper it. Wrap in foil and bake until soft, about 1 hour. Set aside until cool to the touch.

Peel and discard the skin of the eggplant. Puree the eggplant in a blender or food processor until smooth. Set aside.

Squeeze the cloves from the head of garlic into a blender or food processor and puree until smooth. Set aside.

Bring the stock to a simmer in a large kettle. Add the sweet potatoes, potatoes, parsnip, leek, rutabaga, and carrot and cook for 10 minutes or until barely tender. Add the green beans and cook for 5 to 7 minutes. Add the zucchini and chard and cook for 3 minutes more. Just before serving, fold in the eggplant puree and all of the garlic puree. Serve in large heated bowls (I like bistro bowls for this; see note on page 53). Combine the lemon zest and parsley and garnish each serving with about 1 teaspoon of the mixture.

Note: There is no oil in this soup. However, I like to pour a teaspoon or so of a lemon oil from Italy over the finished soup just as I serve it. There are many such oils on the market at specialty foods stores, but my favorite by far is Agrumato Extra Virgin Olive Oil Pressed with Lemons imported by Manicaretti, Inc., in South San Francisco (415-589-1120). A real winner!

Infused Oils— the New Kitchen Basic

The lemon oil I usually add to the Winter Pot-au-Feu with Pureed Eggplant and Roasted Garlic and used in the Chanterelle Lasagne with Lemon Oil is a marvel of instant flavor enhancement. Opulent truffle oil is the wonder-worker in Hubert Keller's Succulent Truffled Potato Stew. These are only two of the many versatile flavored oils flooding the market today. These products—like the concentrated vegetable broths and vinaigrettes replacing traditional heavy meat stocks—form part of a revised vocabulary of contemporary cooking, providing a means of packing deep, vibrant flavor into dishes from which excessive amounts of butter, cream, eggs, or hydrogenated oils have been deleted in the interest of good health.

Whether or not you are interested in cutting anything out of your cooking, these condiments are a pleasure to use. Just a few drops of an herb- or spice-infused oil may be all that's necessary to season a whole dish, transform a soup from flat to vivid, or enliven a vinaigrette. For example, a bit of juniper oil may bring out the best in a pork chop, roasted chili oil intensifies the warmth of a southwestern stew, porcini oil underlines the woodsy character of a mushroom-based dish, and basil oil complements a green fettuccine. Besides working well as the base for butter, cream, or stock sauces, flavored oils are terrific when added to vegetable sautés or stir-fries. They produce exceptional salad dressings, mayonnaises, and marinades for meat, poultry, and fish. The herbed oils are wonderful for drizzling over pizza and focaccia and make a simple but lovely dipping sauce for pieces torn off a crusty loaf of bread. The citrus oils—lime, orange, lemon—make handy substitutes for fresh zest; a scant ½ teaspoon is the approximate equivalent of 1 tablespoon of grated zest.

Of the herb-flavored oils, those infused with mint, basil, or cilantro are the subtlest and most versatile, while the resinous and intense thyme, rosemary, and oregano offerings should be used more sparingly. Non-olive-oil-based infusions like the concentrated citrus oils and Asian sesame, ginger, and peanut oils are particularly potent. Go easy.

There's a wealth of infusions to choose from, but the Consorzio line of flavored olive oils developed by chef Michael Chiarello of the Napa Valley's famed Ristorante Tra Vigne is especially good and widely available at gourmet shops as well as Williams-Sonoma stores, or you can order directly from Napa Valley Kitchens (800-288-1089). I particularly like the Consorzio porcini oil. Although the Agrumato lemon oil from Italy is hard to resist (see note with Winter Pot-au-Feu with Pureed Eggplant and Roasted Garlic), you can prepare a good, economical version by following this simple method from Michael Chiarello.

MICHAEL CHIARELLO'S CITRUS-FLAVORED OIL

MAKES ABOUT ½ CUP

This method results in an oil that captures the fresh flavor of citrus. Look for fruit with thin skins—the more pith, the more bitter the flavor. If you can find only fruit with thick skins, see the note at the end of the recipe. Orange is a knockout, but try tangerines and kumquats, too. You can also make an oil with both orange and lemon, though I prefer the clear flavor of the single fruit.

2 **medium oranges or 3 lemons, Meyer lemons, or limes, cut into eighths**
2 **cups olive oil**

Roughly chop the fruit—skins, seeds, and all—in a food processor with short pulses or with a chef's knife. Do not process to a puree. If the fruit is too finely chopped, the oil will emulsify with the pulp and not separate. Transfer the fruit to the work bowl of an electric mixer and add the oil. Mix on low speed for 10 minutes with the paddle attachment. Let stand at room temperature for 2 hours.

Rinse 4 layers of cheesecloth in cold water and squeeze dry. Suspend a fine-mesh strainer over a fat separator or bowl. Put the citrus mixture in the cheesecloth and squeeze to extract the oil. (As you squeeze, the web of cheesecloth loosens. The strainer will catch the bits of pulp that may escape.) Let stand again to allow the oil and juice to separate. The clear oil will float above the thick mixture of juice, pulp, and some emulsified oil. Pour the oil off into a sterilized glass jar or bottle and discard the juice. Cover tightly, refrigerate, and use within 1 week.

Note: If the fruit has thick skin, the pith may add some bitterness to the oil. To avoid this, peel the zest with a vegetable peeler, put in a food processor, and chop finely. Cut the pith off the fruit, being careful not to cut into the pulp. You want to save as much juice and pulp as possible. Cut the fruit into eighths and process with the zest. Then put in the mixer and mix as directed.

Bistro Bowls

A good investment for the table are bistro-style bowls. These make a dramatic presentation for cassoulet, pot-au-feu, and other slightly soupy dishes. I like the white ones with a diameter of 10 to 12 inches and a generous, shallow bowl. Available from the Williams-Sonoma catalog, where they are listed as "brasserie tableware" (P.O. Box 7456, San Francisco, CA 94120; 800-541-2233).

Roast Corn and Chili Gazpacho

SERVES 6

My enthusiasm for the refreshing "liquid salad" of Spain was reignited when I thought to toss in smoky corn that had been roasted right in the husk on the grill.

2	cups of fresh corn kernels scraped from 6 medium ears of corn
4	vine-ripened tomatoes, about ½ pound, seeded and diced
1	yellow bell pepper, seeded and diced
1	European cucumber, peeled, seeded, and diced
1½	celery ribs, diced
1	serrano chili, seeded and minced
1	medium-large red onion, diced
2	garlic cloves, minced
1	cup V-8 juice
1	tablespoon red wine vinegar
1	tablespoon balsamic vinegar
1	tablespoon fresh lime juice
1	tablespoon olive oil
2	tablespoons chopped parsley
2	tablespoons chopped cilantro plus cilantro leaves for garnish
½	teaspoon ground cumin
	Worcestershire sauce to taste
1½	teaspoons salt or to taste
	Freshly ground black pepper to taste
	Crème fraîche for garnish

Prepare a barbecue for grilling.

Pull down the leaves of the corn without detaching, remove the silk, and rewrap the leaves up around the kernels. Soak the corn in water for several minutes. Place the ears on the grill rack and roast over medium-hot coals,

ROAST CORN AND

CHILI GAZPACHO

•

TUNISIAN BRIKS À LA NIÇOISE

•

STRAWBERRIES IN LEMON

VERBENA WITH FRESH CHEESE

ICE CREAM

WINE SUGGESTIONS:
A CRISP OREGON PINOT GRIS
OR A SPANISH VINO VERDE

turning frequently, for about 10 minutes or until done. Cool, then husk the ears and cut the corn from the cobs, catching as much corn milk as possible.

Combine the corn, tomatoes, yellow pepper, cucumber, celery, chili, and onion in a large nonreactive bowl; toss to combine. Set aside a third of the vegetables. Place the remaining vegetable mixture in a blender. Add the garlic and puree. Add the V-8 juice, vinegars, lime juice, olive oil, parsley, cilantro, and cumin; puree.

Transfer to a bowl and add the reserved vegetables. Season to taste with the Worcestershire sauce, salt, and pepper. Cover and refrigerate for several hours. Serve well chilled in soup bowls or mugs garnished with crème fraîche and a few cilantro leaves.

Minestrone with Rosemary-Chili Pesto

The chili contributes a nice spicy bite to this easy-to-prepare soup. Unlike other pestos, this one is superlight, containing not a drop of oil. The soup has an iron constitution, adapting readily to almost any vegetable you may have on hand.

2	tablespoons olive oil
1	large onion, finely chopped
1½	cups finely chopped celery
2	cups finely shredded cabbage
1½	cups finely chopped carrot
2	quarts low-sodium or homemade chicken or vegetable stock or water
1	cup cannellini beans, soaked in cold water overnight, rinsed, and drained
½	cup small pasta
1	cup finely diced zucchini
½	pound green beans, trimmed and cut into ½-inch pieces

Rosemary-Chili Pesto

½	packed cup chopped parsley
2	tablespoons tomato paste
2	tablespoons fresh rosemary needles
2	garlic cloves, minced
¼	cup pine nuts, lightly toasted
1¼	cup freshly grated Parmesan cheese (4 ounces)
1	small green chili such as serrano, seeded and minced

Heat the oil in a large heavy saucepan over medium heat, add the onion and celery, and sauté until soft, about 3 to 4 minutes. Add the cabbage and carrot and cook until soft, about 5 minutes. Add the stock and beans and simmer over low heat, covered, for 30 minutes. Add the pasta, zucchini, and

green beans and cook for about 10 to 15 minutes more or until the beans and other vegetables are tender.

To make the Rosemary-Chili Pesto, combine the parsley, tomato paste, rosemary, garlic and nuts in a blender or food processor and blend until finely chopped. Add the cheese and chili and process the pesto to a dry paste.

Just before serving, swirl the pesto into the soup and stir over low heat for 2 minutes. Ladle into warm soup bowls.

Mexican Hot and Sour Soup with Hominy

Serves 6

Wine suggestions:
A medium-bodied beer or a
French Côtes-du-Rhône
or a California Zinfandel
with forward fruit

A delicious soup with tantalizing flavor and addictive appeal. The inspiration for it comes from the Wappo Bistro and Grill in Calistoga, California, where innovative chef-owners Michelle Mutrux and Aaron Bauman work a distinctive culinary terrain all their own, combining elements from South American and Mediterranean cuisines. Theirs is some of the best food I have tasted in northern California.

Michelle says she unearthed the broth that forms the basis of this recipe in a very old Mexican cookbook. She and Aaron serve the soup with sautéed meatballs and almonds, but I like this all-vegetable version, too.

1   teaspoon vegetable oil
3   chipotles (smoke-dried jalapeño chilies), seeds and
      stems removed, or 1 to 2 tablespoons chopped
      canned chipotles *en adobo*
2   cups torn-up dry bread
3   garlic cloves, peeled
⅓   cup red wine vinegar
1   pound fresh tomatillos, husked
1   quart chicken or vegetable stock, preferably homemade
1   14½-ounce can hominy, drained, about 1½ cups
1   medium ripe tomato, seeded and chopped
½   pound green beans, trimmed and cut into ½-inch pieces
2   medium carrots, coarsely chopped
⅓   cup shredded Muenster cheese
1   small ripe avocado, cubed
3   small corn tortillas, toasted and cut into strips
      Chopped fresh marjoram
      Chopped fresh cilantro leaves
      Lime wedges

In a sauté pan coated with the oil, lightly toast the chilies over medium heat until aromatic and slightly softened, about 2 minutes. In a food processor fitted with the metal blade, finely grind the chilies. Add the bread, garlic, and vinegar and process into a thick paste.

In a separate saucepan, cover the tomatillos with water and simmer until softened and tender, about 8 minutes. Drain, add to the chili mixture, and puree until smooth.

Transfer the puree to a saucepan and dilute with the stock. Stir to blend. Add the hominy, tomato, green beans, and carrots and simmer for 15 to 20 minutes.

To serve, put a little of the shredded cheese into each bowl, pour the hot soup over the cheese, and garnish with chopped avocado, some tortilla strips, and herbs. Serve the lime wedges on the side.

Springwater Mushroom Broth

This is the recipe of Tom Stokey, the owner of Noodles, a small home-made pasta take-out shop in St. Helena just below my office. I often have this light, flavorful soup for lunch or take some home as a first course for dinner. The red pepper flakes deliver a touch of heat.

¼ cup dry white wine
1 cup vegetable or chicken stock, preferably homemade
1 teaspoon cumin seeds
2 garlic cloves, minced
¼ teaspoon hot red pepper flakes
2 quarts springwater
1 pound white mushrooms, thinly sliced
4 to 6 fresh shiitake mushrooms, sliced
1 red bell pepper, seeded and finely chopped
½ pound angel hair pasta, optional
    Salt to taste
3 scallions, both white and green parts, minced

In a saucepan, heat the wine, stock, cumin seeds, garlic, and red pepper flakes. Simmer for 2 minutes.

Add the springwater, mushrooms, and bell pepper. Simmer for 30 minutes more. If you wish, cook the pasta in the stock just before serving. Add salt and garnish with the scallions.

WHITE BEANS AND FENNEL AU PISTOU

SERVES 4

The pounded mixture of basil and garlic we know as pesto migrated in the late nineteenth century from Genoa to Provence, where it became *pistou*. The French love to mix its classic pungent flavor into other vegetables and vegetable soups. The presence of anise-flavored Pernod clearly marks this recipe as Provençal.

I turn these beans into a quick lunch by adding some canned Italian tuna. For a more formal presentation I like to ladle the bean pistou into bistro bowls (see box on page 53) and top each serving with a piece of broiled or grilled swordfish, tuna, or bass.

2	cups dry white beans such as cannellini or Great Northern, soaked 4–6 hours or overnight and drained
1	fennel bulb, trimmed and thinly sliced
¼	cup olive oil
2	medium ripe tomatoes, peeled
1	garlic clove
1	cup fresh basil leaves
¼	cup parsley leaves
	Salt and freshly ground black pepper to taste
¼	cup light Pernod

Rinse the beans with fresh water. In a large pot cover the beans with 6 cups of salted water. Let simmer, uncovered, for 35 to 40 minutes, or until the beans are soft, but not mushy. In a medium skillet, sauté the fennel in 2 tablespoons of the olive oil until tender but not browned, about 5 minutes. Add the beans and set aside.

In a blender or food processor, puree the tomatoes, garlic, basil, and parsley with the remaining olive oil. Season with salt and pepper.

When you're ready to serve, reheat the beans, whisk in the *pistou* and Light pernod, and cook until hot. If you're not serving the fish, you may like the beans with a little Parmesan cheese grated on top.

WHITE BEANS AND FENNEL

AU PISTOU

•

ROASTED ASPARAGUS WITH

SOFT-COOKED QUAIL EGGS

AND TAPENADE

•

RHUBARB COBBLER

WINE SUGGESTIONS:

A RED CÔTES DE PROVENCE

OR A CALIFORNIA PINOT NOIR

Borscht with Cabbage and Apples

Wine suggestions:
A dry German Riesling
(Trocken) or a rounder
Alsatian Riesling

My version of this substantial soup owes its inspiration to the late Eugenia Doll, a New York hostess famous for her Russian food and extraordinarily generous spirit. It was her idea to add pureed tomato and apples to the classic beet-flavored soup of her homeland. Serve the soup hot or cold but always topped with sour cream and some chopped fresh dill. I think it's best made with the Golden Veal Stock.

You can cook the beets and potatoes a day ahead.

8	medium-large beets, cooked and peeled
4	medium russet potatoes
2	tart apples, cored and coarsely chopped
2	cups fresh or canned crushed tomatoes
1	tablespoon balsamic vinegar
1	tablespoon fresh lemon juice
1	tablespoon sugar
3	quarts veal, chicken, or vegetable stock, preferably homemade
1	small head of cabbage, cored and shredded
	Finely grated zest of 1 lemon
½	cup chopped fresh dill
2	cups sour cream

Julienne 6 of the beets and set aside.

Boil or steam the potatoes in their skins until tender but not mushy. Cool slightly, peel, and julienne. Set aside.

In a small saucepan over medium-high heat, cook the apples in the tomatoes until soft, about 15 minutes. Cool and puree in a blender or food processor with the 2 remaining beets, vinegar, lemon juice, and sugar until smooth.

In a large soup pot, bring the stock to a simmer, add the puree and shredded cabbage, and cook for 15 minutes.

Add the julienned beets and potatoes, return the soup to a simmer, and cook over low heat until heated through.

Add the lemon zest and chopped dill and serve at once with the sour cream passed separately.

BOUILLABAISSE OF FENNEL AND POTATO

SERVES 6

Just as authentic as its better-known cousin, the splendid fish soup of Marseilles, a bouillabaisse of vegetables is delicious in its own right and a lot easier to make. This rustic version features fennel, but you can make equally good ones built around peas or spinach.

I like to serve this as a light lunch with a poached egg on top or as a first course with a garnish of roughly chopped, vine-ripened tomatoes and a soft-cooked quail egg.

Arthur Gold and Robert Fizdale, two friends whose delight in cooking from the garden did much to deepen my own, introduced me to the all-vegetable bouillabaisse, and this recipe is based on one of theirs.

1   quart chicken or vegetable stock, preferably homemade
3   pinches of saffron threads
1   medium onion, chopped
1   fennel bulb, trimmed and finely chopped, feathery
      greens reserved
¼   cup olive oil
3   medium russet potatoes, peeled and thinly sliced
2   garlic cloves, finely chopped
2   tablespoons light Pernod
    Salt and freshly ground black pepper to taste
    Croutons: 6 ½-inch-thick slices French bread, lightly
      toasted and brushed with melted butter or olive oil
    Poached or hard-cooked eggs, fennel greens, and
      tomato *concassée* for garnish

In a large soup pot, bring the chicken stock to a simmer. Add the saffron, turn off the heat, cover, and let the saffron steep in the hot stock for about 10 minutes.

In a skillet, sauté the onion and fennel in the oil over low heat, stirring often, until limp but not brown, about 4 to 5 minutes. Add the chicken stock, potatoes, garlic, light Pernod, and salt and pepper. Cover, bring to a boil, lower the heat, and simmer for about 10 minutes more.

To serve, place a crouton in each warmed soup bowl, carefully place a poached egg on the crouton, ladle the soup over it, and sprinkle with some chopped fennel greens. For a lighter version, omit the crouton and garnish servings with chopped hard-cooked eggs and a spoonful of tomato *concassée*.

Tangy Greens and Wheatberry Soup

I treasure sorrel for its high-acid tang, but if you can't find it, watercress, dandelion greens, Swiss chard, and other assertive greens make good substitutes. Remember to soak the wheatberries overnight, or you'll be cooking the soup for a very long time. The roasting of these unprocessed whole kernels imparts a pleasing, nutty taste. Combining the two stocks gives just the right body to the soup. For a lighter soup, use only chicken stock.

2	cups wheatberries
¼	pound pancetta, chopped, optional
2	medium onions, finely chopped
1	garlic clove, minced
1	cup diced carrot
½	pound shiitake or porcini mushrooms, cleaned and sliced
1	cup finely diced celery
1	medium tomato, peeled, seeded, and chopped
½	teaspoon fennel seeds, crushed
½	teaspoon hot red pepper flakes
	Salt to taste
1	quart homemade or low-sodium canned chicken stock
1	quart beef or veal stock, preferably homemade
2	cups coarsely chopped sorrel
1	cup crème fraîche, sour cream or low-fat yogurt

Toast the wheatberries on a baking sheet in a 350°F oven for about 10 minutes. Cool. Place in a large bowl, cover with cold water, and soak overnight. Drain.

In a large heavy saucepan, cook the pancetta over medium-high heat until browned, about 4 minutes. Add the onions, garlic, carrot, mushrooms, celery, and tomato. Cover loosely and cook, stirring occasionally, until the vegetables are tender, about 5 minutes. Stir in the wheatberries, fennel seeds, red pepper flakes, and salt.

Add the stocks, raise the heat to high, and bring to a boil. Lower the heat and simmer until the wheatberries are tender, about 15 minutes. Add the sorrel and cook for 5 to 10 minutes more or until it is wilted and tender. Stir in the crème fraîche and serve at once.

Double Celery Soup with Apple and Dill

Serves 6

This is a mellow combination with a guess-the-ingredient depth of flavor.

2   **medium yellow onions, diced**
2   **medium celery root bulbs, peeled and diced**
2   **medium bunches of celery, chopped**
½   **cup unsalted butter**
1   **quart homemade or low-sodium canned chicken stock**
2   **green apples, such as Granny Smith, cored**
¼   **cup chopped fresh dill**

In a partially covered heavy saucepan, sauté the onions, celery root, and celery in the butter over low heat, stirring occasionally, until soft but not browned, about 10 to 15 minutes. Cool. Add the stock and puree in a blender until smooth. Return the puree to the saucepan.

Grate or finely dice the apples.

Heat the soup thoroughly. Serve it in warm bowls with some of the grated apple and a sprinkling of chopped dill.

COLD CUCUMBER SOUP WITH DILL

Here is another soup recipe from Hubert Keller, chef and owner of Fleur de Lys in San Francisco. For this soup I prefer the long European hothouse cucumbers to the American type, partly because they're less bitter. Leave the peel on, but slice the cukes in half and remove the seeds with a teaspoon. The toasted black mustard seeds add a surprising taste and texture to this light-as-air soup.

2　European cucumbers, seeded and diced, about 5 cups
2　teaspoons fresh dill plus some sprigs for garnish
1　tablespoon Dijon mustard
1½　teaspoons champagne vinegar
¼　cup plain yogurt
　　Salt and freshly ground black pepper to taste
1　bunch of red radishes, finely minced
1　teaspoon black mustard seeds or black sesame seeds,
　　　　toasted for several minutes or until they turn gray
　　　　and begin to pop, then cooled

Puree the cucumber in a blender in several batches. Transfer the pureed cucumber to a large serving bowl. Add the dill, mustard, vinegar, yogurt, salt, and pepper. Return to the blender in batches and puree until smooth. Transfer back to the bowl, cover, and chill for at least 1 hour.

Just before serving, stir half of the minced radish into the soup. Ladle the soup into individual serving bowls and garnish with the remaining radish, some toasted mustard seeds, and, if you like, a sprig of dill.

WALNUT AND ROASTED RED
PEPPER PÂTÉ
•
SAVORY WINE BISCUITS
•
COLD CUCUMBER SOUP WITH
DILL
•
TENDER CORN CAKES WITH
GOAT CHEESE, WATERCRESS
SAUCE, AND SMOKED SALMON
•
PINEAPPLE CRUMBLE

WINE SUGGESTIONS:
A CALIFORNIA SÉMILLON OR A
DRY WHITE BORDEAUX

Mostly Vegetable Side Dishes

Leaves of Brussels Sprouts with Chestnuts

Cabbage with Lemon and Tarragon

Dilled Carrots with Capers

Carrots with Aniseed

Sformato of Carrots

Sformato of Cauliflower with Tomato-Watercress Concassée

Baked Belgian Endive

Fava Beans à la Grecque

Stir-Fried Asian Greens

Green Beans with Mustard Seeds and Almonds

Mashed Potatoes with Leeks

Rösti (Swiss Skillet Potatoes)

Sweet Potato Puree with Aromatic Spices

Roasted Pearl Onions and Shallots

Italian-Style Stuffed and Roasted Peppers

Savory Baked Ricotta

Gingered Spinach with Cilantro

Tomato Aspic with Saffron-Herb Mayonnaise

Shredded Zucchini Salad

Zucchini with Cilantro

Beets with Red Currants

Red Cabbage with Pears

Carrots with Cranberries and Dill

Rutabagas with Golden Delicious Apples

Leaves of Brussels Sprouts with Chestnuts

Wine suggestions:
A Gigondas or a medium-
bodied California
Rhône blend

Frankly, chestnuts are a pain to roast and peel, but they impart a flavor like no other nut. Until recently the only alternative has been canned chestnuts imported from France, but these are expensive and lacking in flavor. A much better choice are the new vacuum-packed peeled and roasted chestnuts in pouches now available at fancy-food groceries.

Separating the brussels sprout leaves takes a bit of patience, but on the plate the result looks incredibly delicate—like a mound of lily pads. And they're not just pretty; the taste is almost delicate as well. Even people who protest that they don't like brussels sprouts adore them prepared this way. This dish is wonderful served with the Wild Mushroom Bread Pudding.

8   cups brussels sprout leaves, about 2 to 3 pounds
½   cup chicken stock, preferably homemade
1   cup coarsely chopped roasted chestnuts
1   teaspoon minced fresh thyme
    Salt and freshly ground black pepper to taste

With a sharp knife, trim the end off each sprout; discard along with any tough outer leaves. Gently separate the leaves and set aside enough to make 8 cups. You may need to continue trimming the bottom as the leaves get closer to the core. Discard the cores.

In a large saucepan over medium-high heat, cook the sprout leaves in the chicken stock, covered, for about 4 to 5 minutes. Add the chestnuts, thyme, salt, and pepper. Cook, tossing gently, until the chestnuts are just heated through.

CABBAGE WITH LEMON AND TARRAGON

This is an excellent accompaniment for grilled salmon and teams beautifully with Rösti (Swiss Skillet Potatoes). If you use the yogurt, the dish is low in fat; I sauté the cabbage in wine instead of the usual butter.

1   medium green cabbage, cored and thinly sliced
1   small yellow onion, sliced
1   cup dry white wine
    Salt and freshly ground black pepper to taste
    Grated zest and juice of 1 lemon
1   garlic clove, minced
1   cup crème fraîche or low-fat yogurt
¼   cup Dijon mustard
2   tablespoons chopped fresh tarragon

In a large covered skillet over medium heat, cook the cabbage and onion in the wine along with a generous pinch of salt for about 10 minutes.

Add the lemon zest, juice, garlic, and crème fraîche, cover, and cook for another 10 minutes. Add the mustard and tarragon and cook for a few minutes more. Season with salt and pepper and serve at once.

CABBAGE WITH LEMON AND

TARRAGON

•

RÖSTI (SWISS SKILLET

POTATOES)

•

CARROTS WITH CRANBERRIES

AND DILL

•

ROAST APPLE CRÈME BRÛLÉE

WITH GRAVENSTEIN CAKE

WINE SUGGESTIONS:
AN OFF-DRY
GERMAN KABINETT OR
CALIFORNIA RIESLING

DILLED CARROTS WITH CAPERS

This is a simple and straightforward preparation with a dash of Italian flavor. For less fat, blanch or steam the carrots or omit the butter before cooking in the liquid of your choice.

WINE SUGGESTIONS:
A RICH, LIGHTLY OAKED
CALIFORNIA CHARDONNAY OR
A CALIFORNIA VIOGNIER

3   tablespoons unsalted butter
2   pounds young carrots with ferny greens attached,
        peeled, ½ inch of stem left on
    Salt and freshly ground black pepper to taste
1   cup chicken stock, preferably homemade, white wine,
        or apple cider
2   tablespoons drained capers
2   tablespoons minced dill

In a saucepan large enough to hold the carrots, melt the butter. Add the carrots, a pinch of salt, and the stock. Cover and cook over low heat for 15 minutes or until tender. Add the capers and dill and mix gently. Season with salt and pepper and serve.

CARROTS WITH ANISEED

SERVES 6

The uncommon tastes of aniseed and light Pernod complement the sweetness of the buttery carrots. This is very French.

1	**pound carrots, sliced about ½ inch thick on the diagonal**
	Salt to taste
2	**tablespoons unsalted butter**
¼	**teaspoon aniseed, lightly toasted and ground**
1	**teaspoon light Pernod**
2	**tablespoons chopped fresh parsley**

In a medium saucepan, combine the carrots, salt, and enough cold water to cover. Bring to a simmer and cook for 10 to 15 minutes or until barely tender.

Drain the carrots and return them to the saucepan, adding the butter, aniseed, and light Pernod. Gently cook over low heat, stirring frequently, until the butter is melted. Serve immediately, decorated with parsley.

ESCAROLE-SHALLOT-APPLE
TARTE TATIN

•

FARCI WITH FRESH
WHITE CHEESE

•

PARSLEY AND MINT SALAD

•

CARROTS WITH ANISEED

•

FRESH FRUIT WITH
GOOD SPIRITS

•

LAVENDER SHORTBREADS

WINE SUGGESTIONS:
A FRESH WHITE WINE FROM
HAUTE-SAVOIE OR AN
OREGON PINOT GRIS

Sformati of Vegetables

These old-fashioned dishes from Italy put leftover cooked vegetables to use in an elegant way. *Sformato* means "unmolded," and any sformato is first cooked in a mold before it is turned out, pretty and delicate, onto a warm serving plate. Almost any vegetable or combination of vegetables will take to this treatment. Sformati can be eaten separately as a first course or made the focal point of a luncheon.

SFORMATO OF CARROTS

This dish is slightly sweet, and the *quatre épices* gives it a hint of pumpkin-pie taste.

2	cups cooked sliced carrots
1	tablespoon unsalted butter
1½	tablespoons all-purpose flour
1	cup half-and-half
3	large eggs, separated, at room temperature
¼	teaspoon *quatre épices*
2	tablespoons freshly grated Parmesan cheese
1	teaspoon salt
½	teaspoon freshly ground black pepper

Preheat the oven to 375°F. Butter and lightly flour a 2-quart soufflé dish or charlotte mold or six 1-cup individual molds.

Puree the cooked carrots in a blender or pass through a food mill until smooth.

In a heavy saucepan, melt the butter over medium heat. Add the flour and cook, stirring, for 1 minute. Remove from the heat and, with a wire whisk, stir in the half-and-half, whisking until the mixture is smooth. Bring to a boil, stirring constantly, then cook for 1 minute more. Cool slightly, then whisk in the egg yolks, spice mixture, cheese, salt, and pepper until well blended. Add the pureed carrots and mix well.

Beat the egg whites until stiff but not dry. Gently fold a small amount of the egg whites into the carrot mixture, then fold the carrot mixture into the egg whites. Pour the mixture into the prepared mold, set the mold in a *bain marie* (water bath), and bake for about 45 minutes for large molds and 30 minutes for small molds or until a tester inserted into the center comes out clean.

Unmold onto a serving plate or individual serving plates and serve at once.

WARM BEET SALAD WITH

WALNUTS AND DILL

•

SFORMATO OF CAULIFLOWER

WITH TOMATO-WATERCRESS

CONCASSÉE

•

SFORMATO OF CARROTS

•

CHIVE POPOVERS

•

DRIED FRUIT WITH

GOOD SPIRITS

WINE SUGGESTIONS:
ROSSO DI MONTALCINO OR A
CALIFORNIA SANGIOVESE OR A
LIGHT- TO MEDIUM-BODIED
ZINFANDEL

SFORMATO OF CAULIFLOWER WITH TOMATO-WATERCRESS CONCASSÉE

SERVES 6

Roquefort is a great flavor companion for cauliflower. This *sformato* makes an excellent starter or main course for lunch.

Concassée is the French term for something that is chopped roughly or pounded in a mortar. In culinary usage it usually refers to tomatoes that have been peeled, seeded, and chopped. Fresh tomato *concassée*, an un-cooked sauce of coarsely chopped tomatoes, makes a piquant topping for cooked vegetables, pasta, or fish. Serve at once.

2	tablespoons unsalted butter
1	garlic clove, peeled and smashed
2	cups cooked cauliflower
2	large shallots, minced
1½	tablespoons all-purpose flour
1	cup half-and-half
	Salt and freshly ground black pepper to taste
6	large eggs, separated, plus 2 egg whites at room temperature
2	ounces Roquefort cheese, about ¼ cup, crumbled

Concassée

1	bunch of watercress, chopped
2	medium ripe tomatoes, seeded and diced
1	large garlic clove, minced
	Juice of 1 lemon
¼	cup virgin olive oil
	Salt and freshly ground black pepper to taste

Preheat the oven to 375°F. Use 1 tablespoon of the butter to grease a 2-quart soufflé dish or charlotte mold. Rub all over with the smashed garlic.

Puree the cooked cauliflower in a blender until smooth or pass through a food mill. Melt the remaining butter in a heavy saucepan over medium heat, add the shallots, and sauté until wilted but not browned, about 5 minutes. Add the flour and cook, stirring constantly, for 1 minute. Remove from the heat and add the half-and-half. Return to the heat and cook, stirring, until the mixture is completely smooth. Season with salt and pepper.

Stir in the cauliflower along with the egg yolks and cheese. Correct the seasoning with additional salt and pepper.

Beat the egg whites until stiff but not dry. Gently fold a small amount of the egg whites into the cauliflower mixture, then fold the cauliflower mixture into the egg whites.

Pour the mixture into the prepared mold set in a *bain-marie* (water bath), and bake for about 30 minutes or until a tester inserted into the center comes out clean. Let the *sformato* sit for a minute, then run a knife around the edges and unmold it onto a warm serving plate.

To make the *concassée*, toss the watercress, tomatoes, and garlic with the lemon juice and olive oil in a small bowl. Season with salt and pepper. Serve the *sformato* topped with 2 tablespoons of the *concassée*.

Variations: Substitute cooked and pureed broccoli for the cauliflower and Parmesan cheese for the Roquefort or make a *sformato* of peas, substituting prosciutto for the cheese. Spinach all by itself is good seasoned with a little nutmeg. Invent your own combinations.

What Is a Vegetable?

The primary definition for *vegetable* is simply "a plant." But then what about fruits? Are some foods vegetables and fruits at the same time? Well, it depends on who's talking. Botanists say a fruit is anything that derives from a flower's ovary and contains one or more seeds. According to this definition, many vegetables shift over to the fruit tribe. Here are some examples of botanical fruits that are culinary vegetables:

TOMATOES	CUCUMBERS	PEPPERS
EGGPLANTS	CORN KERNELS	WINTER AND SUMMER SQUASHES
GREEN BEANS	OKRA	SNOW PEAS
AVOCADOS	PUMPKINS	OLIVES

BAKED BELGIAN ENDIVE

A great dish for company, this will not suffer if left to cook a bit longer than planned when the cocktail hour runs long. Any excess bitterness is held in check by the sugar and lemon juice and, of course, all that lovely butter.

The slightly bitter taste of the endive makes this an excellent companion for the Vegetable Risotto with Carrot, Celery, and Parsley Broth. Also good as a light luncheon entree for 4.

4	**tablespoons unsalted butter**
3	**pounds Belgian endive, cut lengthwise into quarters, ends trimmed**
1	**teaspoon sugar**
	Juice of ½ lemon
	Salt and freshly ground black pepper to taste
	Freshly minced parsley for garnish

Preheat the oven to 375°F. Butter a shallow 9- by 13-inch baking dish with 1 to 2 tablespoons of the butter.

Arrange the endive in a single layer, packing it tightly. Season with the sugar, lemon juice, salt, and lots of pepper. Cut the remaining butter into small pieces and dot over the endive. Cover with foil and bake for 40 minutes, basting several times. Remove the foil, baste again, increase the oven temperature to 425°F, and bake for 15 minutes more or until the endive is soft. Decorate with parsley just before serving.

BAKED BELGIAN ENDIVE

•

CHANTERELLE LASAGNE WITH

LEMON OIL

•

DILLED CARROTS WITH CAPERS

•

PARSLEY AND MINT SALAD

•

ROAST APPLE CRÈME BRÛLÉE

WITH GRAVENSTEIN CAKE

WINE SUGGESTIONS:

A RICH, LIGHTLY OAKED

CALIFORNIA CHARDONNAY OR A

CALIFORNIA VIOGNIER

Chicory for Winter

Belgian endive (called *Witloof chicory* in England) is a member of an esteemed though rather complicated tribe of plants—the chicories. Radicchio is another member of this aristocratic family. They are greens I particularly like in winter. All make a decided difference when added to salads, where they impart their unique texture and pronounced astringency, a property that is, for some, something of an acquired taste. Braised in butter, they are excellent on their own or served as a foil for other vegetable dishes.

Most chicories are blanched by growers—shielded inside a mound of soil and straw—to whiten them and to keep out the sunlight that intensifies their natural bitterness. It's a difficult crop for the home gardener, who must first take nearly a season just to grow the roots that will then be pulled, stored, and replanted in a darkened environment before they produce a leafy plant of the proper pallor. When buying endive (and now you know why it's so costly), select crisp, creamy white heads with little or no discoloration. If you're lucky, you might find some still cocooned in their crates in the traditional heavy royal-blue paper that protects them from the light. It's a pretty sight.

There are two other chicories you will want to mix into your winter greens: the curly, or cut-leaf, endive called *frisée* and the broader-leafed escarole.

FAVA BEANS À LA GRECQUE

SERVES 6

I grew up eating a lot of lima beans in the South, and I still love them. The fava bean, however, has a good deal more respectability at the moment, and so, bowing to the winds of fashion, I make this salad using favas instead of their humble American cousin. The shaved cheese at the end is the idea of Bruce Le Favour, a great friend, great neighbor, and renowned chef.

When you see the words *à la Grecque* on a menu, you're probably not contemplating a dish of Greek origin. The phrase refers to a simple French technique for preparing vegetables for cooling salads or appetizers, a refreshing treatment any time of the year. Vegetables cooked *à la Grecque* are first simmered in an aromatic broth of oil, herbs, lemon, seasonings, and water, then removed from the broth and chilled. The broth is boiled down to concentrate its flavor and poured over the cooled vegetables. Mushrooms are most often selected for this preparation, but fennel, artichoke hearts, cucumber, cauliflower, endive, bell peppers, and small white onions are other good candidates. Favas, or limas, are my favorite.

FAVA BEANS À LA GRECQUE

•

RISOTTO WITH SWEET CORN

•

CATAHOULA'S TOMATOES-IN-
ALL-THEIR-GLORY SALAD

•

STRAWBERRIES IN LEMON
VERBENA WITH FRESH CHEESE
ICE CREAM

WINE SUGGESTIONS:
A CALIFORNIA CHARDONNAY
OR A FRENCH MEURSAULT

2   **pounds fresh young fava beans* or fresh lima beans, shelled**
2   **teaspoons paprika**
2   **garlic cloves, chopped**
1   **bay leaf**
6   **black peppercorns**
¼   **cup olive oil**
    Juice of 1 lemon, plus 6 very thin lemon slices, seeds removed
    Salt and freshly ground black pepper to taste
    Pinch of cayenne pepper
3   **tablespoons chopped fresh parsley or chervil**
    Lemon oil, homemade or store-bought, for garnish
6   **ounces Pecorino Romano cheese, shaved**

Put everything except the parsley, lemon oil, and cheese in a saucepan. Add just enough water to cover. Cook, uncovered, over low heat for about 10

Mostly Vegetable Side Dishes   83

minutes or until the beans are barely tender; do not drain. Cool, then refrigerate overnight. Drain, reserving the cooking liquid and reducing it in a small saucepan to a thick syrup over high heat, about 5 minutes.

Divide the beans among 6 salad plates, drizzle some of the reduced sauce over each serving, garnish with the parsley, and drizzle on a little lemon oil. Top with the cheese shavings and some freshly ground pepper.

*Favas, called *broad beans* in Britain and *fèves* in France, are an early-crop bean sold in Italian markets, farmers' markets, and sometimes supermarkets in the spring and early summer months. If the ones you find are on the mature side, they may be tough unless you go to the trouble of first peeling off the outer skins.

STIR-FRIED ASIAN GREENS

SERVES 6

In China the word for "vegetable" is the same as the word for "cabbage"—
choi. The three greens suggested for this stir-fry are all members of the
brassica, or cabbage, family, but none is sharp-tasting or cabbagey. Tatsoi is
a flat cabbage, almost rosette shaped, with tender, fleshy leaves that taste
rather like spinach.

This dish makes a delicious accompaniment to the Wild Rice Pancakes
or the Roasted Barley and Wild Mushroom Pilaf.

¼ **cup dry white wine**
¼ **cup water or homemade or low-sodium canned
       chicken stock**
1   **tablespoon sugar**
1   **tablespoon soy sauce**
½ **teaspoon hot or plain sesame oil**
1   **teaspoon cornstarch**
1   **tablespoon vegetable oil**
1   **garlic clove, minced**
1   **teaspoon grated fresh ginger**
½ **pound shiitake mushrooms, stemmed and sliced**
2   **pounds mixed Asian greens, such as bok choy, Chinese
       broccoli, and tatsoi**

In a small bowl, combine the wine, water, sugar, soy sauce, sesame oil, and
cornstarch. Stir well to combine and set aside.

Heat the vegetable oil in a wok over medium heat. Add the garlic and
cook until very aromatic, about 1 minute; do not let it color or burn. Add
the ginger and mushrooms, raise the heat to medium-high, and stir-fry until the mushrooms begin to soften, about 2 minutes. Add the greens and
cook, covered, until they begin to wilt, about 2 to 3 minutes more.

Add the wine-stock mixture to the greens and bring to a boil. Cook uncovered, stirring frequently, until the sauce thickens and the vegetables are
well coated, about 3 minutes more.

WILD RICE PANCAKES

•

STIR-FRIED ASIAN GREENS

•

TANGY GREENS AND

WHEATBERRY SOUP

•

PEARS BAKED IN CREAM

WINE SUGGESTIONS:
A FRUITY GERMAN MÜLLER-
THURGAU OR AN OFF-DRY
CALIFORNIA RIESLING

Green Beans with Mustard Seeds and Almonds

Hot, spicy garden beans with lots of texture and crunch. The grinding together of the uncooked peas and rice is very Indian. These go especially well with the Sweet Potato Puree with Aromatic Spices and pair nicely with Catahoula's Tomatoes-in-All-Their-Glory Salad for a light summer lunch.

This dish is just as good at room temperature as it is warm, so you can make it ahead for use as part of a vegetable buffet.

1	pound green beans, trimmed and cut into ¼-inch pieces on the diagonal
1	tablespoon dried yellow split peas
1	tablespoon white rice
2	hot green chilies, such as jalapeños or serranos, seeded and minced
3	tablespoons water
4	tablespoons unsalted butter
3	tablespoons finely chopped almonds or cashews
1	teaspoon black mustard seeds
¼	teaspoon curry powder
1	teaspoon salt or to taste
	Freshly ground black pepper to taste
3	tablespoons chopped fresh dill

Steam the green beans for 6 to 8 minutes or until crisp-tender. Set aside.

Grind the split peas and rice to a powder in a spice mill or clean coffee grinder.* Transfer to a small mixing bowl, add the chilies and water, and mix well.

Heat the butter in a large skillet over medium heat. When it begins to foam, add the almonds and fry for 15 to 20 seconds or until they just begin to brown. Add the mustard seeds and fry until they just begin to pop, about 30 seconds. Add the curry powder and the pea mixture. Cook until dry, about 5 minutes.

Add the steamed green beans, salt, and pepper. Sauté, stirring and shaking the pan until the beans are heated through. Remove from the heat, add the dill, and serve.

*Have 2 grinders—one for coffee, one for spices.

Starters

THAI-INSPIRED
SEAFOOD SALAD

CANTALOUPE
WITH BLACK
OLIVES

TUNISIAN BRIKS À
LA NIÇOISE

Spring & Summer

CATAHOULA'S TOMATOES-IN-ALL-THEIR-GLORY WITH CORN WAFFLES

COLD CUCUMBER SOUP WITH DILL

GOAT CHEESE CAKE

ASIAN SESAME NOODLE SALAD

ITALIAN-STYLE STUFFED AND ROASTED PEPPERS

SHREDDED
ZUCCHINI
SALAD

CARROT-RHUBARB
SOUP WITH
CINNAMON
CROUTONS

ROASTED
ASPARAGUS WITH
SOFT-COOKED
QUAIL EGGS
AND TAPENADE

OLIVE MOUSSE

SFORMATO OF
CARROTS

CILANTRO MOUSSE

SFORMATO OF
CAULIFLOWER

TOMATO ASPIC

SFORMATO OF
CARROTS

SFORMATO OF CAULIFLOWER WITH
TOMATO-WATERCRESS CONCASSÉE

OLIVE MOUSSE

TOMATO ASPIC

SFORMATO OF
CARROTS

Fall & Winter

BEETS WITH
RED CURRANTS

ESCAROLE-
SHALLOT-APPLE
TARTE TATIN

RÖSTI
(SWISS SKILLET
POTATOES)

CHANTERELLE
LASAGNE WITH
LEMON OIL

ROASTED PEARL
ONIONS AND
SHALLOTS

MUSTACHE-OF-
THE-DRAGON
WHEATBERRY
PILAF

PASTA SAUCE
WITH BEAN
SPROUTS, GREENS,
SHIITAKE
MUSHROOMS,
AND SESAME
SEEDS

Desserts

ROASTED APPLE
CRÈME BRÛLÉE

BANANA-
COLADA TART

TUSCAN FIG
AND BREAD TART

MASHED POTATOES WITH LEEKS

SERVES 10

These potatoes are not low-fat, but they are truly delicious.

1 **bunch of leeks, about 4 medium, white parts only, split in half lengthwise, rinsed well, and dried**
   Salt to taste
10 **russet or other starchy potatoes, peeled and quartered**
6 **tablespoons unsalted butter**
½ **cup cream**

In a saucepan, boil the leeks in enough salted water to barely cover until tender, about 5 minutes; drain.

In a large saucepan, simmer the potatoes in heavily salted water over medium-high heat until tender, about 20 minutes. Drain, reserving 1 cup of the water. Put the cooked potatoes through a ricer or mash them by hand, adding the butter and cream and enough of the potato water to make a smooth paste.

Place the leeks in a blender with a little of the remaining potato water; puree until smooth. Fold into the potato puree.

Though best eaten right away, this dish may be made ahead and kept warm over a double boiler or reheated in the microwave on high power for 2 minutes.

TOMATO ASPIC WITH SAFFRON-
HERB MAYONNAISE

•

SEA BASS BAKED ON A BED OF
ARTICHOKES, ASPARAGUS,
AND SHALLOTS

•

MASHED POTATOES
WITH LEEKS

•

CARDAMOM SHORTBREAD
COOKIES

•

FIGS IN ARMAGNAC

WINE SUGGESTIONS:
A CRISP CALIFORNIA
CHARDONNAY OR AN ITALIAN
CORTESE DI GAVI

Rösti (Swiss Skillet Potatoes)

SERVES 6 TO 8 AS A SIDE DISH OR 4 AS A MAIN COURSE

One of the best foods of all time is a crusty fried potato pancake traditional in the workingman's cafés of Switzerland. The excellent recipe for rösti (skillet potatoes) in the cookbook of my dear friends and mentors, Arthur Gold and Robert Fizdale (*The Gold and Fizdale Cookbook,* Random House, 1984), formed the basis for my experimentation with this deceptively simple specialty. Arthur and Bobby were themselves inspired by research into the subject by the great Swiss chef Fredy Girardet.

Although the only ingredients are potatoes, onions, salt, and butter, this dish is highly susceptible to variation, and reproducing it is something of a trick. Precooking the potatoes is a must if you want a moist, creamy center and a golden crust. The secret lies in the type of potatoes you select and how long you precook them. High-starch baking-type potatoes like russet and Yukon Gold are good choices. Parboil the potatoes in their skins until barely tender or until a fork will just pierce the center.

I like rösti served plain as a side dish or on its own with sour cream and crumbled bacon as it's served in some parts of Switzerland. Rösti is good topped with a soft-cooked egg, dusted with almost any minced fresh herb, or sprinkled with shredded cheese. Just about anything goes.

You will need two 10-inch nonstick skillets, two 9-inch heat-resistant dinner plates, and a good flexible spatula.

3	**large starchy potatoes, such as russets**
½	**cup minced shallot or onion**
12	**tablespoons unsalted butter (1½ sticks)**
	Salt and freshly ground black pepper to taste
2	**tablespoons cold water**

Wash the potatoes and boil them in their skins until just tender, about 20 minutes. Peel them and dry them in a pot over low heat for a minute or two. Set aside to cool.

Sauté the shallot in 2 tablespoons of the butter in a small skillet over medium heat until wilted but not browned, about 3 minutes. Transfer the shallot and butter to a large bowl. Grate the potatoes coarsely with a grater (*not* in a food processor, or they will be too wet). Add them to the shallot.

Melt 2 more tablespoons of the butter and pour it over the potato mixture. Gently combine the potatoes and shallots and season with salt and pepper.

Divide the remaining butter (8 tablespoons) between two 10-inch non-stick skillets and heat until foaming. Divide the potato mixture between the skillets and spread it out in an even layer, pressing down with the back of a spoon. Sprinkle 1 tablespoon cold water over each skillet and cover with an inverted heatproof plate. Cook the rösti over medium heat, shaking the skillets from time to time. After 15 minutes, gently raise the edge of a pancake to see if it is browning properly. When the bottoms are golden brown, carefully loosen the pancakes all around. Remove the skillets from the heat. Cover with the warmed plates and invert the rösti onto them. Slide the pancakes back into the skillets and brown the other sides for about 10 minutes. Remove from the pans and serve at once.

Sweet Potato Puree with Aromatic Spices

I love to work with intriguing spice combinations, and I often turn to the cuisine of India for inspiration. Most of its exotic flavorings already reside on your pantry shelves or can be turned up with no trouble at the local market. It's the artful blending of these familiar ingredients that makes for the unexpected.

3	pounds sweet potatoes, cooked and peeled
3	tablespoons unsalted butter
2	teaspoons fennel seeds, crushed
1	teaspoon cardamom seeds, crushed
2 to 3	tablespoons light brown sugar or maple syrup
½	teaspoon grated orange zest
¼	cup fresh orange juice
1	teaspoon salt or to taste
	Juice of 1 lime
¼	cup lightly toasted freshly grated coconut

Puree the sweet potatoes in a food processor or using a potato ricer.

In a large skillet, melt 2 tablespoons of the butter over moderate heat. When it begins to foam, add the crushed fennel and cardamom seeds. Stir quickly, then add the potato puree, brown sugar, orange zest, orange juice, and salt. Cook, stirring frequently, until thickened, about 5 minutes. Squeeze in the lime juice and add the remaining butter. Garnish each serving with the toasted coconut.

ROASTED PEARL ONIONS AND SHALLOTS

SERVES 6

This is an excellent garnish for almost any dish.

20	ounces (2 pint boxes) pearl onions
½	pound shallots
2	tablespoons olive oil
	Salt and freshly ground pepper to taste
2	tablespoons fresh thyme leaves or 1 tablespoon dried

Preheat the oven to 350°F. Lightly oil a baking dish.

Arrange the onions and shallots in their skins in the baking dish in one layer. Drizzle on the oil, sprinkle with salt and thyme, and bake for about 35 to 40 minutes or until they are soft. Allow to cool for a few minutes; gently slip from the skins. (The onions and shallots may be prepared to this point several hours in advance and reheated in a microwave-safe baking dish, covered, on full power for 2 minutes, just before serving.) Season with salt and pepper and add a little more thyme if you wish.

GRILLED STUFFED FIGS AND

APRICOTS

•

MUSTACHE-OF-THE-DRAGON

WHEATBERRY PILAF

•

BEETS WITH RED CURRANTS

•

ROASTED PEARL ONIONS

AND SHALLOTS

•

CHOCOLATE PUDDING CAKE

WINE SUGGESTIONS:

A PROVENÇAL WHITE CASSIS OR

A LIGHT CALIFORNIA

SAUVIGNON BLANC

Italian-Style Stuffed and Roasted Peppers

SERVES 6

This rustic Italian version of the meat-filled American standard first appeared from the inimitable Elizabeth David in her classic *Italian Food* (Macdonald, 1954), packs fresh tomatoes, garlic, and anchovies into glowing red and yellow pepper cases. Make extra because these are always a hit. Serve them with lots of good bread such as focaccia to soak up the precious juices spooned over the peppers at the last minute.

6 **large red or yellow bell peppers or pimento or a mixture of both**
Salt and freshly ground black pepper to taste
6 **garlic cloves, peeled**
6 **medium ripe tomatoes, peeled, quartered, and seeded**
16 **anchovy fillets, rinsed, dried, and split, oil reserved**
Olive oil, enough for 3 tablespoons when combined with reserved anchovy oil
Coarsely chopped fresh parsley for garnish

Preheat the oven to 375°F. Lightly oil a shallow roasting dish.

Cut the peppers in half lengthwise, remove the seeds and veins, but leave the stems intact to help the pepper halves hold their shape. Lightly salt the inside of the pepper halves. Using a garlic press, squeeze 3 of the garlic cloves and divide among the pepper halves.

Arrange the peppers in a single layer in the roasting dish. Tuck the tomato quarters into the halved peppers peeled side up; try to pack 3 or 4 quarters tightly into each half since they shrink as they bake. Divide the anchovies and remaining garlic, thinly sliced, among the peppers. Spoon the olive-anchovy oil over the peppers, season with pepper, and roast, uncovered, for 30 to 45 minutes or until the peppers are tender and toasted around the edges.

Pour all the pan juices over the peppers, garnish with the chopped parsley, and serve.

Italian-Style Stuffed and Roasted Peppers

•

Savory Baked Ricotta

•

Shredded Zucchini Salad

•

Tuscan Fig and Bread Tart

Wine suggestions:
Montepulciano d'Abruzzo
or a Chianti Classico Riserva
or try a California
Sangiovese or Nebbiolo

SAVORY BAKED RICOTTA

There are certain recipes I am particularly partial to, and this is one of them—so simple, so open to variation, and so good with so many things that I make it over and over again. Sometimes I toss fresh herbs into the ricotta mixture before baking it or use flavored oils like hot pepper or truffle oil in place of the olive oil. For dessert I omit the oil and drizzle honey over the cheese, accompanying each serving with some raspberries and sweet ripe peaches.

This savory version of the dish teams beautifully with the Italian-Style Stuffed and Roasted Peppers.

3   **large egg whites**
½   **teaspoon salt**
2   **cups ricotta cheese***
     Olive oil

Preheat the oven to 375°F.

In a bowl, beat the egg white with salt until soft peaks form. Fold the ricotta into the egg whites until well blended. Pour the mixture into 6 lightly oiled ½-cup custard cups. Pour a little olive oil over each one.

Bake for 30 minutes. The ricotta will rise, then settle when cool. Unmold and serve slightly warm or at room temperature, never chilled.

*Fresh sheep's milk ricotta from an Italian specialty store or cheese shop tastes best, but supermarket ricotta will do perfectly well.

ITALIAN-STYLE STUFFED AND
ROASTED PEPPERS

•

SAVORY BAKED RICOTTA

•

SHREDDED ZUCCHINI SALAD

•

TUSCAN FIG AND BREAD TART

WINE SUGGESTIONS:
MONTEPULCIANO D'ABRUZZO
OR A CHIANTI CLASSICO RISERVA
OR TRY A CALIFORNIA
SANGIOVESE OR NEBBIOLO

Gingered Spinach with Cilantro

SERVES 6

A warmly fragrant spinach puree with a hint of Indian spice. It goes well with the Sweet Potato Puree with Aromatic Spices.

1	gallon water
	Salt to taste
3	pounds fresh spinach
1	teaspoon finely grated fresh ginger
1	teaspoon finely minced garlic
1	teaspoon finely minced hot green chilies, such as serrano or jalapeño
1	teaspoon salt
½	cup finely chopped cilantro
3	tablespoons olive oil
¼	cup raw cashews or almonds, coarsely chopped

Preheat the oven to 350°F. Lightly grease a medium ovenproof or microwave-safe dish.

Bring the water and some salt to a boil in a large kettle and plunge the spinach into it. When the water returns to a boil, cook the spinach for 2 to 3 minutes or until well wilted. Drain, squeezing out as much water as possible.

In a blender or food processor, combine the spinach, ginger, garlic, chili, 1 teaspoon salt, cilantro, and 2 tablespoons of the olive oil and blend to a smooth paste. Pour into the greased baking dish.

In a small skillet, heat the remaining oil over medium heat. Toss the nuts in the oil and fry them, stirring constantly, until they just begin to color, about 2 minutes. Stir the nuts into the spinach mixture and bake for 20 minutes or until heated through. Or cover and refrigerate for several hours, then bake for 30 minutes.

Tomato Aspic with Saffron-Herb Mayonnaise

SERVES 6 TO 8

I couldn't write a vegetable cookbook without including this favorite dish from my childhood in the South. Aspics are out of favor, but I find them a wonderfully cool and refreshing first course on the hottest days of summer. Served with a little crabmeat or shrimp on the side, a pretty tomato aspic conjures up pictures of an old-fashioned ladies' luncheon—white gloves, polished silver, spacious verandas, and long, trailing arms of Spanish moss moving in the distance.

1	quart fresh tomato juice
2	tablespoons gelatin
2	celery ribs, finely diced
1	tablespoon finely minced onion
1	teaspoon salt
1	tablespoon minced fresh basil
⅛	teaspoon cayenne pepper
1	tablespoon grated orange zest
3	tablespoons fresh orange juice

Saffron-Herb Mayonnaise

1	large egg
1	teaspoon salt
1	teaspoon freshly ground black pepper
3	tablespoons fresh lemon juice
1	teaspoon Dijon mustard
2	cups light fruity olive oil
¼	teaspoon crumbled saffron threads, dissolved in 2 teaspoons warm cream
2	cups minced fresh herbs, such as chives, basil, tarragon, parsley, and/or chervil

Butter lettuce leaves for serving

TOMATO ASPIC WITH

SAFFRON-HERB MAYONNAISE

•

SEA BASS BAKED ON A BED OF

ARTICHOKES, ASPARAGUS,

AND SHALLOTS

•

MASHED POTATOES

WITH LEEKS

•

CARDAMOM SHORTBREAD

COOKIES

•

FIGS IN ARMAGNAC

WINE SUGGESTIONS:
A CRISP CALIFORNIA
CHARDONNAY OR AN ITALIAN
CORTESE DI GAVI

**Vine-ripened tomatoes, quartered, black olives,
radishes, and chive blossoms for garnish**

In a saucepan, heat ½ cup of the tomato juice, add the gelatin, and stir vigorously to dissolve. When the gelatin is dissolved, remove from the heat and stir in the remaining aspic ingredients.

Rinse a 4-cup ring mold with cold water and pour in the aspic mixture. Cover and refrigerate for about 2 hours or until set.

To make the mayonnaise, place the egg, salt, pepper, lemon juice, and mustard in a food processor or blender. With the motor running, add the oil in a steady stream until all is incorporated, remove from the bowl, and stir in the dissolved saffron and minced herbs.

To serve, dip the bottom of the mold in warm water for a few seconds and invert onto a serving platter lined with butter lettuce leaves. Heap the mayonnaise in the center and serve with fresh tomato quarters, a few black olives, crisp radishes, and lavender chive blossoms.

SHREDDED ZUCCHINI SALAD

SERVES 6

A combination of green and golden zucchini varieties works well in this wonderful hot-weather side dish.

3	medium-large zucchini, about 1¼ pounds, cut into long thin strands*
2	tablespoons unseasoned rice wine vinegar
3	tablespoons extra-virgin olive oil
	Salt and freshly ground black pepper to taste
¼	cup lightly toasted pine nuts
2	tablespoons thin ribbons of basil
2	ounces Parmesan cheese, thinly shaved

Drain the zucchini in a colander for about 20 minutes; gently squeeze to remove excess water.

Place the zucchini in a large serving bowl. Add the vinegar, oil, salt, and pepper and mix well. Just before serving, gently toss in the pine nuts, basil, and cheese.

*Although I'm not a big fan of kitchen gadgets, I am positively in love with a turning vegetable slicer I recently discovered in a Japanese housewares store in San Francisco. This Asian device magically converts battalions of squash, beets, potatoes, and other potentially overproductive vegetables into thin-as-rice-noodle julienne strands. (I can't prove it, but I believe that the cutting of vegetables into different shapes actually affects the way they taste.) You can have one of these miracle tools in your home kitchen for a price. The turning-slicer is made by the Benriner Company and is available for about $90 from J. B. Prince Co. (212-302-8611). I've used the Benriner Slicer for years; this is its second cousin.

SHREDDED ZUCCHINI SALAD

•

GRILLED TUNA WITH SAFFRON

VINAIGRETTE

•

GOAT CHEESE CAKE AND

SALAD OF MIXED GREENS

•

FRESH FRUIT WITH

GOOD SPIRITS

•

LAVENDER SHORTBREADS

WINE SUGGESTIONS:
A FRENCH POUILLY-FUMÉ
OR A MEDIUM-BODIED
CALIFORNIA SAUVIGNON BLANC

Zucchini with Cilantro

SERVES 4

The sharp tastes of ginger and cilantro really liven up the delicate flavor of this most adaptable of summer squashes.

2   garlic cloves, minced
1   tablespoon grated fresh ginger
1   tablespoon unsalted butter
1   pound zucchini, thinly sliced
¼   teaspoon salt
2   tablespoons roughly chopped cilantro leaves
⅔   cup plain yogurt

In a medium skillet, sauté the garlic and ginger in the butter over medium heat for 2 minutes or until soft but not browned. Add the zucchini and cook, covered, for about 3 minutes more. Season with salt. Gently fold in the cilantro leaves and yogurt. Serve at once.

Wine suggestions:
An Alsatian Pinot Blanc or
an off-dry California
Riesling

All Together Now: Fruits and Vegetables

In savory cooking I like to pair fruits and vegetables in side dishes to accompany such sturdy main courses as gratins and risotti. The balance of sweetness and acidity in the fresh fruit can mellow or spark a recipe in a special way, providing a tanginess that works in pleasant contrast to the luxuriance of potato- or grain-based dishes, and does it without adding a lot of extra ingredients.

The fruit-vegetable marriage is quite common in the cuisines of Europe, particularly in France, where such dishes accompany roast meats and game, but it has never really caught on here, which is too bad. These cousins in the produce world have a synergistic effect; combining them uncovers complex flavor affinities you'd never guess. The absolute master of the form, legendary cook Josephine Araldo, learned much of her fruit-with-vegetable art from her Breton grandmother, who foraged fresh ingredients from garden, arbor, trellis, orchard, woodland, and field. She combined at the optimum moment the discovered vegetables, fruits, mushrooms, and herbs in original "found" dishes at once rustic and refined. Cabbage with blueberries is a typical Araldo admixture, spinach with green plums another. The following four recipes represent a few of my own favorite pairings. I hope you will try them and be moved to invent harmonious combinations of your own.

Beets with Red Currants

The fruit and the vegetable combined in this dish make a natural duo; currants are loved best in cold-weather parts of the world like Scandinavia and Russia, exactly where beets are most prized. Our own supermarkets consider this fruit too fussy to handle, so search for the bright berries in specialty markets. Their clean tang is indispensable to the recipe. Make this in the spring and early summer, when currants are fresh and the new beets ready. Pomegranate seeds can be substituted for the currants.

2 **pounds beets, cooked**
1½ **tablespoons light brown sugar**
1 **teaspoon water**
 Juice of 1½ oranges, about ½ cup
3 **tablespoons unsalted butter**
1 **pound fresh red currants or fresh pomegranate seeds**
 Dash of pastis or other anise-flavored liqueur
 Salt and freshly ground black pepper to taste
 Fresh dill sprigs for garnish

Peel the beets and slice them into julienne pieces.

Put the sugar and water into a small heavy saucepan or skillet and heat it over medium heat until the sugar begins to caramelize. Add the orange juice and butter and cook briefly, until you have a thick syrup.

Set aside 6 little bunches of currants for decoration and stem the rest.

Add the beets to the orange syrup and stir to coat evenly. Cook over medium-low heat for 3 to 4 minutes, stirring constantly. Add the currants and cook for a minute more. Remove from the heat, add the pastis, and season with salt and pepper.

Divide the beets among 6 plates and garnish each serving with a bunch of currants and a sprig of dill.

RED CABBAGE WITH PEARS

SERVES 6

This is adapted from *From a Breton Garden: the Vegetable Cookery of Josephine Araldo,* (Aris Books, 1990). Sometimes I use radicchio in place of the red cabbage. When I do, I lengthen the cooking time by 15 minutes.

2	tablespoons unsalted butter
1	garlic clove, peeled and cut in half
1	red cabbage, cored and thinly sliced
½	cup dry red wine such as Merlot or Cabernet Sauvignon
½	teaspoon coarse salt
2	underripe pears, peeled, cored, and sliced ¼ inch thick
1	yellow onion, thinly sliced
⅛	teaspoon *quatre épices* (page 136)
	Salt and freshly ground black pepper to taste
⅓	cup water
1	tablespoon light brown sugar
¼	pound Gorgonzola or other blue cheese

Grease a large heavy flameproof casserole with the butter and rub it with the garlic.

In a large nonaluminum bowl, combine the cabbage, wine, and coarse salt; toss and let stand for at least 1 hour.

Drain the cabbage, reserving the marinating liquid. Layer the cabbage, pears, and onion in the prepared dish, sprinkled with the spice mixture, salt, and pepper, until everything is used up. Pour the marinating liquid and water over all and sprinkle with the brown sugar. Cook, uncovered, over low heat for about 2 hours or until all the liquid is absorbed and the cabbage is quite soft.

Crumble the cheese on top just before serving.

SPRINGWATER

MUSHROOM BROTH

•

RÖSTI (SWISS SKILLET POTATOES)

•

RED CABBAGE WITH PEARS

•

RED ONION MARMALADE

•

ORANGE-YOGURT CORNMEAL CAKE

WINE SUGGESTIONS:
A CALIFORNIA MERLOT OR A MERITAGE RED BLEND

CARROTS WITH CRANBERRIES AND DILL

SERVES 6

WINE SUGGESTIONS:
A FRUITY RED CÔTES-DU-
RHÔNE OR A CALIFORNIA
ZINFANDEL. IF YOU ARE SERVING
THIS AROUND THANKSGIVING,
TRY A NEWLY RELEASED
BEAUJOLAIS NOUVEAU.

"The Indians and English use them much," observed an early visitor to New England of the wild cranberries that grew in abundance from North Carolina to Nova Scotia. These native crimson fruits have far too short a season, so freeze or dry them for year-round use or seek out dried berries in natural foods stores. A good mail-order source, American Spoon Foods of Petoskey, Michigan, will send you its own cranberries, dried without sulfites, at about $8.50 a pound (800-222-5886). Rehydrate dried cranberries by cooking them in a small saucepan with hot water or juice until tender. Soaking first, then simmering, produces a more tender fruit.

2 pounds baby carrots, peeled
½ cup dried cranberries
½ cup apple cider
2 tablespoons unsalted butter
   Salt and freshly ground black pepper to taste
1 tablespoon minced fresh dill

In a large skillet over medium-high heat, cook the carrots and cranberries in the cider, covered, until just tender, about 12 minutes. Add the butter, reduce the heat to medium, and toss the carrots and cranberries until glazed. Season with salt, pepper, and dill.

RUTABAGAS WITH GOLDEN DELICIOUS APPLES

In this dish earthy yet dimly sweet rutabagas are both lightened and refined by the presence of apples. If you can find them, quince or Fuji apples are wonderful in place of Golden Delicious.

3	tablespoons unsalted butter
4	large rutabagas, peeled and cut into ½-inch dice, about 8 cups
¼	cup water
2	large Golden Delicious apples, peeled, cored, and cut into ½-inch dice, about 2½ cups
	Persillade: 2 tablespoons finely chopped parsley mixed with 1 minced garlic clove, 1 teaspoon grated lemon zest, and 1 tablespoon minced fresh tarragon
	Salt and freshly ground black pepper to taste

In a skillet, melt the butter over medium heat. Add the rutabagas and water and cook, covered, stirring occasionally, for about 15 minutes or until tender. Add the apples, cover, reduce the heat to medium-low, and cook until tender, about 10 minutes more. Add the persillade and season with salt and pepper. Toss well and serve at once.

SPRINGWATER

MUSHROOM BROTH

•

CELERY ROOT AND

PARSNIP GRATIN

•

RUTABAGAS WITH GOLDEN

DELICIOUS APPLES

•

ENDIVE AND WATERCRESS

SALAD WITH ORANGES

AND FENNEL

•

PEARS BAKED IN CREAM

WINE SUGGESTIONS:
A FRESH FRENCH VOUVRAY OR
AN OFF-DRY CALIFORNIA
CHENIN BLANC

Mostly Vegetable Main Courses _____

Stuffed Artichokes

Roasted Asparagus with Soft-Cooked Quail Eggs and Tapenade

Cauliflower with Lentils in a Spiced Tomato Sauce

Chanterelle Lasagne with Lemon Oil

Roasted Barley and Wild Mushroom Pilaf

Celery Root and Parsnip Gratin

Mustache-of-the-Dragon Wheatberry Pilaf

Cod Baked in Parchment with Chermoula-Couscous Crust

Sea Bass Baked on a Bed of Artichokes, Asparagus, and Shallots

Tender Corn Cakes with Goat Cheese, Watercress Sauce, and Smoked Salmon

Risotto with Lemon and Herbs

Vegetable Risotto with Carrot, Celery, and Parsley Broth

Risotto with Sweet Corn

Vegetarian Cassoulet

Wild Mushroom Bread Pudding

Farci with Fresh White Cheese (Farci au Fromage Blanc)

Grilled Tuna with Saffron Vinaigrette

Hubert Keller's Succulent Truffled Potato Stew with Pâté à L'Eau

Gratin of Potatoes and Fennel with Rouille

Eggplant Torte with Fresh Tomato Compote

Speedy Pasta Meals from Simple Sauces

Artichoke Hearts Picante

Pasta Sauce with Cauliflower, Anchovies, Garlic, and Hot Red
Pepper Flakes

Pasta Sauce with Tuna, Capers, Olive, and Tomato

Pasta Sauce with Tapenade, Orange Zest, Olives, and Cheese

Pasta Sauce with Walnuts, Garlic, Bread Crumbs, Cheese, and Parsley

Pasta Sauce with Pancetta, Shallots, Golden Raisins, Rosemary, and
Balsamic Vinegar

Pasta Sauce with Bean Sprouts, Greens, Shiitake Mushrooms, and
Sesame Seeds

STUFFED ARTICHOKES

In *The Food of France,* Waverley Root writes that Haute-Provence is not a place you fall in love with at once but rather slowly, unconsciously, until your affection becomes "unshakable." Artichokes are an emblematic food of this region and, along with lavender, olive, and misty thyme, seem wrung from its pale, subtly hued landscape.

These artichokes are extraordinarily good, best eaten at room temperature or slightly warm. When served with a ferocious aïoli and some crusty bread, they constitute a complete robust meal all on their own.

2	lemons
1	quart cool water
8	medium-large artichokes, about ½ pound each
3	cups bread crumbs from good crusty French or Italian bread
10	garlic cloves, peeled
1	2-ounce can anchovies packed in oil, fillets drained and patted dry
¼	cup minced parsley
¼	cup olive oil
4	cups thinly sliced onion, about 2 pounds
2	green bell peppers, seeded and cut into thin strips
2	red bell peppers, seeded and cut into thin strips
2	ripe but firm tomatoes, peeled and diced
1	tablespoon chopped fresh thyme leaves
1	tablespoon chopped fresh tarragon leaves
	Salt and freshly ground black pepper to taste

Preheat the oven to 350°F.

Remove the zest from one of the lemons, mince it, and set aside. Combine the juice of one lemon with the water in a large nonreactive bowl.

Cut away the tough, spiny outer leaves on each artichoke. Using a knife, cut 1½ to 2 inches off the tops of the artichokes. Peel the stems and trim so the artichokes will sit flat. Use a small spoon to scoop and scrape out the

BOUILLABAISSE OF FENNEL

AND POTATO

•

STUFFED ARTICHOKES

•

MIXED GREENS WITH

TAPENADE VINAIGRETTE

•

MODESTE AUX CERISES

WINE SUGGESTIONS:
A YOUNG ITALIAN BARBERA
D'ALBA OR CALIFORNIA PINOT
NOIR

fuzzy chokes and place the prepared artichokes in the acidulated water until you're ready to cook.

Over medium-high heat, toss the bread crumbs in a nonstick pan until lightly toasted. Mash 4 of the garlic cloves with the anchovies and half of the parsley to make a paste. Add the lemon zest and combine with the bread crumbs. Evenly divide the stuffing among the artichokes, packing it gently into the cleaned centers.

In a large ovenproof casserole, heat the olive oil. Add the onion, peppers, tomatoes, remaining garlic cloves, sliced, herbs, and the juice from the remaining lemon. Braise, uncovered, over medium heat for 15 minutes, stirring often, until the vegetables are soft but not browned. Season with salt and pepper.

Arrange the artichokes over the bed of vegetables. Cover with a lid or first with a layer of wax paper or greased parchment and then with foil. (Never let foil come directly in contact with artichokes; it will discolor them.) Bake for 1 hour, adding up to ½ cup water if needed. If the artichokes appear dry while baking, baste them with the cooking juices. They are done when the tip of a knife easily pierces the center.

Cool to room temperature before serving. Decorate with additional minced parsley if you wish. Or, for something a little different, dust with chermoula on page 120.

Roasted Asparagus with Soft-Cooked Quail Eggs and Tapenade

Roasting intensifies the flavor in vegetables just as it does in meat. Asparagus prepared this way is especially good, and the method is foolproof when you're cooking for a crowd. The soft-cooked eggs and cheese are very Italian, the tapenade very Provençal—an unbeatable Mediterranean matchup.

If you're daunted by the idea of peeling a dozen quail eggs at the last minute or can't find them at all (specialty markets and meat markets are your best bets), 6 poached eggs will taste about the same.

2	pounds asparagus, preferably about ½ inch in diameter, trimmed and peeled
¼	cup extra-virgin olive oil
	Sea salt and freshly ground black pepper to taste
¼	pound Parmesan cheese, shaved
1	dozen quail eggs, soft-cooked (about 1 minute) and peeled just before serving
¼	cup tapenade made from black olives

Preheat the oven to 475°F.

Place the asparagus in a single layer in a heavy roasting pan. Pour the oil over the asparagus and turn the spears to coat. Lightly sprinkle with sea salt.

Roast the asparagus for 15 minutes, turning at least once. Transfer to a large serving platter. Cool for 10 minutes, then cover lightly with Parmesan shavings. Cut the eggs in half and scatter them over the cheese. Dot with tapenade and season generously with pepper.

BAKED JERUSALEM ARTICHOKES

WITH HORSERADISH CRÈME

FRAÎCHE AND CHIVES

•

ROASTED ASPARAGUS WITH

SOFT-COOKED QUAIL EGGS

AND TAPENADE

•

SFORMATO OF CARROTS

•

RHUBARB COBBLER

WINE SUGGESTIONS:
A CALIFORNIA SAUVIGNON
BLANC OR A CALIFORNIA
BLANCS DE NOIR SPARKLING
WINE

CAULIFLOWER WITH LENTILS IN A SPICED TOMATO SAUCE

SERVES 6

This dish of warm and exotic flavors can be served hot or cold or anywhere in between. It makes a good luncheon entree accompanied by a cucumber salad and some simple Indian bread, like chapatis or pappadums. Make it a day ahead if you want; it tastes even better then, when the spices have had a chance to come together.

	Salt to taste
1	**large cauliflower (about 3 pounds), trimmed and cored**
2	**cups lentils**
1½	**teaspoons turmeric**
2	**onions, coarsely chopped**
2	**garlic cloves, minced**
4	**tablespoons unsalted butter**
¼	**cup vegetable oil**
5	**whole tomatoes, peeled, seeded, and coarsely chopped**
1	**bay leaf**
¼	**cup tomato juice or water**
2	**teaspoons ground coriander**
½	**teaspoon garam masala**
1	**teaspoon cumin seeds**
1	**hot green chili such as jalapeño or serrano, stemmed, seeded, and cut into thin slivers**
1	**½-inch piece of fresh ginger, peeled and cut into thin slivers**

3 to 4 tablespoons coarsely chopped cilantro or minced parsley
Lime or lemon wedges

Fill a saucepan slightly larger than the cauliflower half full of salted water and bring to a boil over high heat. Place the cauliflower in it, stem end down, cover, and when the water returns to a boil, simmer for 10 to 15 minutes or until the cauliflower is tender but firm when pierced with a fork. Do not overcook, or it will be mushy in the final dish. (Or steam the cauliflower for 20 to 30 minutes.)

Meanwhile put the lentils and ¾ teaspoon of the turmeric in a pot of salted water and cook according to package directions or until al dente.

While the lentils and cauliflower are cooking, make the tomato sauce. In a medium saucepan, sauté the onions and garlic in 2 tablespoons of butter and 2 tablespoons of oil over medium heat until soft but not browned, about 3 minutes. Add the tomatoes, bay leaf, and tomato juice. Stir to blend.

When the lentils are cooked, drain them and add them to the tomato mixture along with the coriander, garam masala, and remaining turmeric. Cook, uncovered, over medium heat for 10 minutes more. Discard the bay leaf.

Drain the cauliflower and separate into florets. In a separate saucepan, heat the remaining butter and oil and in it sauté the cumin seeds, chili, and ginger over medium heat for 2 to 3 minutes. Add the cauliflower and stir-fry for 4 to 5 minutes or until it begins to turn brown. Add the tomato-lentil mixture, stir gently but thoroughly, cover, and cook over low heat, stirring occasionally for 10 to 15 minutes or until the vegetables are fork-tender. (You may need to add a little water if the vegetables stick to the bottom of the pan, but stir it in gently.) Serve with chopped cilantro or parsley and lemon or lime wedges.

Pappadums

These round paper-thin spiced biscuits made from lentil and rice flours are delectable when nibbled along with a leisurely main course sparked with Indian flavors. Often stocked in the Indian food section of large supermarkets, they are readily found at Indian specialty stores. To cook, just slide them into a skillet containing enough hot but not smoking oil to cover them with ¼ inch of oil. Turn at once and fry for 3 to 5 seconds. Remove and drain on paper.

CHANTERELLE LASAGNE WITH LEMON OIL

This is an elegant dish that sings with lush, well-balanced flavors. It comes from Jerry Comfort, the innovative executive chef at Beringer Vineyards in St. Helena, California. Jerry serves it as a first course, but it's so delicious that I like to make it the main event. Teleme cheese is soft and tangy, perfect for this dish—if you can't find it, the mozzarella/Swiss combination works well too. The Fava Beans à la Grecque are perfect with this.

1½ **pounds chanterelles**
4 **shallots, minced**
4 **tablespoons unsalted butter**
2 **tablespoons water**
 Salt and freshly ground black pepper to taste
1 **pound homemade or store-bought lasagne noodles**
 Oil for the pan
½ **pound Teleme cheese or half mozzarella and half Swiss, sliced**
2 **tablespoons freshly grated Parmesan cheese**
1 **cup homemade or low-sodium canned chicken stock**
 Lemon oil, homemade (page 50) or store-bought
12 **small basil leaves**

Preheat the oven to 400°F. Butter or oil a 9- by 13-inch baking dish.

Clean the chanterelles carefully, setting aside for garnish about 20 small perfect specimens or larger chanterelles cut in half or quartered. Slice the remaining chanterelles.

In a medium skillet, combine 2 tablespoons of the minced shallots, 2 tablespoons of the butter, and the water over medium heat. Add the sliced chanterelles, season with salt and pepper, and cook until the mushrooms are tender and have absorbed all the liquid, about 5 minutes. Remove from the heat, transfer to a food processor, and chop finely. Place in a bowl to cool.

Cook the lasagne noodles according to the package directions or until

BAKED BELGIAN ENDIVE

•

CHANTERELLE LASAGNE
WITH LEMON OIL

•

DILLED CARROTS WITH CAPERS

•

PARSLEY AND MINT SALAD

•

ROAST APPLE CRÈME BRÛLÉE
WITH GRAVENSTEIN CAKE

WINE SUGGESTIONS:
A RICH, LIGHTLY OAKED
CALIFORNIA CHARDONNAY OR A
CALIFORNIA VIOGNIER

barely tender. Remove to a large bowl filled with ice water to prevent further cooking, then transfer to a sheet pan, oiled to prevent sticking.

To assemble the lasagne you will need 9 lasagne noodles. Arrange one layer of the noodles in the prepared dish. Spread half of the chanterelles over them. Top with half of the Teleme cheese and sprinkle with half of the Parmesan. Repeat the layers, top with a final layer of noodles, cover with foil, and bake for 20 minutes or until the cheese begins to melt.

While the lasagne is cooking, sauté the remaining shallots in the remaining butter in the medium skillet, which has been wiped clean, over medium-low heat. Add the reserved chanterelles and the stock, cover, and cook for 3 minutes. Uncover and add the lemon oil and basil leaves.

To serve, spoon about 5 chanterelles and some of the lemon-basil sauce onto each of 6 warm deep plates. Place a generous portion of lasagne at the center of each plate and drizzle with a few drops of lemon oil.

Roasted Barley and Wild Mushroom Pilaf

With barley, mushrooms are a natural accompaniment. Wild mushrooms that taste of the forest—morels, porcini, chanterelles—are best of all, but a combination of cultivated and wild mushrooms also works nicely.

Pan-roasting the barley gives it a marvelous toasty-nutty flavor.

2	**tablespoons olive oil**
2	**cups pearl barley, rinsed**
4	**shallots, minced**
½	**pound assorted wild mushrooms, sliced**
1	**quart homemade veal, chicken, or vegetable stock**
¾	**teaspoon salt or to taste**
	Freshly ground black pepper to taste

2 to 3 tablespoons minced fresh sage

In a large heavy saucepan, heat the oil over medium heat. Add the barley and toast, stirring frequently, for 5 to 8 minutes or until it starts to brown and give off a nutty aroma.

Add the shallots and cook for about 2 minutes. Add the mushrooms and cook until wilted, about 5 minutes. Add 1 cup of the stock and stir until all of it is absorbed. Add the remaining stock and, when it is almost simmering, cover the pan and cook for 45 minutes or until the liquid is absorbed. Add the salt, pepper, and sage and blend them in with a large fork, fluffing the barley. Serve immediately.

Carrot-Rhubarb Soup with Cinnamon Croutons

•

Roasted Barley and Wild Mushroom Pilaf

•

Chiffonade of Radicchio with Baked Goat Cheese

•

Maple Pears with Cardamom Cream

Wine suggestions:
A Spanish Rioja or a medium-bodied California Nebbiolo

Celery Root and Parsnip Gratin

SERVES 6

The traditional gratin is made with potatoes, but there are many versions of this classic dish. Almost any assemblage of root vegetables will produce interesting flavor combinations. Parsnips are one of the most overlooked of the root crops; they look like overgrown anemic carrots but are so sweet when cooked that children mistake them for dessert. To tone down the sweetness, I like to combine them with celery root for some added herbal flavor and a little fresh horseradish for bite.

1	**garlic clove**
2	**tablespoons unsalted butter**
2	**pounds parsnips, peeled and thinly sliced**
1	**pound celery root, about 1 medium, peeled, cut in half, and shredded**
	Salt and freshly ground white pepper to taste
2	**tablespoons freshly grated or bottled horseradish**
1½	**cups heavy cream**
1	**tablespoon minced parsley for garnish**

Preheat the oven to 325°F.

Crush the garlic clove with the back of a wooden spoon and rub it around the inside of a 6-quart gratin or baking dish; discard. Use all the butter to coat the dish.

In a large mixing bowl, season the parsnips and celery root with the salt, pepper, and horseradish. Layer the vegetables in the baking dish and gently press down. Pour the cream over the vegetables.

Bake for 1 hour or until the cream has been reduced by half, breaking the crust formed by the cream several times, forcing new cream to the top. Decorate with parsley just before serving.

Gratins

Favorites of the French, gratins are delectable dishes with a tempting crisp golden-brown crust that can include cheese, bread crumbs, or finely ground nuts. *Au gratin* and *gratinée* simply mean "burned on top." Underneath that thin, tasty crust is a good place to layer hearty vegetables for a warming, substantial midwinter main course.

A classic gratin is served in the dish in which it was cooked—always a shallow oval or round ovenproof container. The best gratin dishes are made of heat-conducting materials like earthenware, cast iron, or copper. The shallowness allows for the largest possible area for the crust. (A sprinkling of paprika helps induce browning.) Some gratin dishes come with small handles to help in transporting piping hot food direct from oven to table.

In Provence a typical dish is the tian, a gratin of layered vegetables laced with oil and *herbes de Provence* and baked in the low oval dish (tian) from which the recipe gets its name. Although in the south of France the tian is often a mixture of classic summer vegetables (tomatoes, zucchini, eggplant), at Christmastime a tian of leeks, Swiss chard, and cardoons (an artichoke relative with a distinctive taste) is traditional when dressed with croutons and an anchovy-flavored cream.

Mustache-of-the-Dragon Wheatberry Pilaf

SERVES 6

Pea shoots—the delicate tendrils and leaves snipped from the growing tips of the podded garden pea—are called "mustaches of the dragon" by the Chinese, who have a penchant for giving their foods lyrical names. Barbara Tropp, author of the definitive *The Modern Art of Chinese Cooking,* is a treasure house of esoterica on Chinese cuisine. She says the ancient river god of China is traditionally depicted as a dragon sporting a wiry, curling mustache with long, tapering ends resembling tendrils. In the twining shoots of the pea plant the Chinese see the mustache of the old river god, and they call this spring specialty by that name. Cooks swirl the jade-colored curls into soups or add them to stir-fries.

Look for dewy-fresh pea shoots (*dau miu* in Cantonese) in spring at Asian, specialty produce, or farmers' markets—or in the pea patch of your own garden. Wheatberries—nutritious unprocessed nuggets of whole wheat—are widely available at natural food stores.

2   **shallots, minced**
3 to 4 **garlic cloves, minced**
2   **tablespoons vegetable oil**
2   **cups wheatberries**
½   **cup dry white wine**
4 to 4½ **cups chicken or vegetable stock, preferably**
        homemade
2   **tablespoons fresh tarragon leaves**
1   **pound pea shoots, coarsely chopped**
     Salt and freshly ground black pepper to taste
     Finely chopped chives for garnish

In a large saucepan, sauté the shallots and garlic in the oil over medium-high heat until soft but not browned, about 4 to 5 minutes. Add the wheatberries and cook, stirring, for a few minutes, until the wheatberries are separated and coated with oil.

Stir in the wine and cook over medium heat, stirring frequently, until the wine has evaporated. Stir in the stock. When the stock reaches a simmer, cover the pan and simmer for 1 hour or more, until the wheatberries are tender and most of the stock is absorbed. Add the tarragon and pea shoots and toss the pilaf until the greens are wilted. Season with salt and pepper and garnish with the chopped chives.

Cod Baked in Parchment with Chermoula-Couscous Crust

Serves 6

The spirited seasonings in the couscous crust are the spices and herbs featured in chermoula, the classic Moroccan sauce. They seem to bring out the best in fish, especially when it is cocooned in parchment paper and baked.

1½ inch piece of fresh ginger, peeled and minced
4   garlic cloves, minced
½   teaspoon ground cumin
¼   teaspoon paprika
⅛   teaspoon cayenne
⅛   teaspoon saffron threads
½   cup chopped fresh cilantro
½   cup chopped flat-leaf parsley
    Juice of 1 lemon
1   small tomato, peeled, seeded, and diced
½   cup olive oil
1   cup couscous
    Salt and freshly ground pepper
1   egg, lightly beaten with 1 teaspoon water
    Flour for dipping
6   5-ounce cod or other firm white fish fillets such
        as sea bass or halibut, about 1 inch thick
    Unsalted butter, melted

Combine all the ingredients except the egg, flour, fish, and butter in a small bowl. Let the mixture stand for 2 hours or overnight in the refrigerator to allow the flavors to develop and the couscous to absorb the oil.

Preheat the oven to 375°F.

To coat the fish, season with salt and pepper. Break the egg and beat with water in a shallow dish. Place flour in another shallow dish, lightly coat each fish fillet with flour, shaking off any excess. Dip into egg, coating completely.

Coat each fish fillet with some of the couscous mixture. Cut 6 rounds of parchment paper about 16 inches in diameter and brush one side of each with melted butter. Place a fillet in the center of each buttered round of paper. Fold the paper over to enclose the fish. Start folding and twisting the edge of the parchment to make a pleated edge all around. Insert a straw into the open end (or blow into it) and fill with air. The airspace allows moisture to rise and fall back on the fish, keeping it very moist. Quickly remove the straw and twist the end of the paper closed tightly.

Place the parchment bundles side by side on baking sheets. Bake for 20 minutes or until the parchment paper is golden brown. Present the fish immediately, or the packets will wrinkle and deflate.

 Southern Parchment Paper

If you don't have parchment paper on hand and can't find any at a kitchen supply store, you can mail-order it from G. B. Ratto and Co. (821 Washington St., Oakland, CA 94607; 800-228-3535 in California, 800-324-3483 elsewhere). Or you can do what my mother and grandmother did in the South: Line your baking pans and baking sheets with pieces of well-greased clean brown paper bags. They work just fine.

Sea Bass Baked on a Bed of Artichokes, Asparagus, and Shallots

Serves 6

The rich-tasting flesh of sea bass is firm, lean, and white. The sea bass caught on the Pacific coast are larger than the East Coast variety and are more often sold as fillets, which is how the fish is used in this recipe.

The idea of a garnish of deep-fried asparagus peelings comes from Jerry Comfort, executive chef at Beringer Vineyards in the Napa Valley.

2	lemons
4	pounds artichokes, about 24 small or 10 to 12 medium
½	cup olive oil
¾	pound shallots, about 18 to 20, peeled
1	tablespoon fresh thyme leaves
1	fresh rosemary sprig
1	pound medium-thick asparagus, trimmed and peeled, ½ cup peelings reserved
6	¼-pound sea bass fillets
1	teaspoon salt
	Freshly ground black pepper to taste
	Vegetable oil for deep-frying

Preheat the oven to 425°F.

To prepare the artichokes, squeeze the juice of one of the lemons into a nonaluminum bowl filled with water, then add the lemon to the water as well. Pull away the outer leaves of each artichoke until the yellow-green center leaves are revealed and discard. Using a stainless-steel knife, trim the stems and any lower leaves and slice off the tips. Slice the trimmed artichokes in half and remove the hairy part of the chokes. Quarter the chokes if they are medium to large. Immediately place each artichoke in the lemon water to minimize discoloration.

In a large heavy nonaluminum casserole (I like enameled cast-iron Le Creuset for this), combine the olive oil, drained artichokes, shallots, thyme, rosemary, and the juice of the remaining lemon. Cover and cook

Wine suggestions:
A crisp California
Chardonnay or an Italian
Cortese di Gavi

over medium-high heat for 8 to 10 minutes. Add the asparagus and toss to combine.

Season the fish fillets generously with salt and pepper. Arrange them on top of the vegetables, cover, and bake for 18 to 20 minutes, depending on the thickness of the fish. Uncover and spoon some of the juices over the fish at least once during cooking. When the fish is cooked, remove the casserole from the oven and let rest, covered, for 3 minutes to allow the fish to firm up.

Just before serving, deep-fry the asparagus peelings in several inches of vegetable oil until crisp and lightly browned. Drain on paper towels.

To serve, arrange a bed of the vegetables on warm plates and place one fillet at the center of each serving. Decorate with 1 tablespoon of crisp asparagus peels.

TENDER CORN CAKES WITH GOAT CHEESE, WATERCRESS SAUCE, AND SMOKED SALMON

SERVES 6

This is my version of a recipe from Hubert Keller, French-born owner-chef of San Francisco's Fleur de Lys restaurant. Hubert creates innovative dishes in every category, but he shines with vegetables, making bright and elegant dishes that fairly shimmer with inspiration. France meets California in these delectable corn cakes, which are also wonderful filled with small pieces of lobster, salmon, or sea scallops.

4 to 6 ears young corn, enough to make 1 pound kernels, or 2 8-ounce cans White Niblets corn, drained
4   large eggs
3   tablespoons all-purpose flour
Salt and freshly ground black pepper to taste
6   ounces goat cheese
Finely chopped chives
2   small bunches of watercress, stemmed
¼   cup olive oil
2   tablespoons chopped shallots
⅓   cup dry white wine
6   tablespoons water
½   cup cream or half-and-half
2   tablespoons peeled, seeded, and diced tomato
Peeled and diced tomato, chervil sprigs, and ¾ pound smoked salmon,* thinly sliced, for garnish

If you're using fresh corn, cook the ears in boiling water or steam them for 2 to 3 minutes until tender, then quickly dip them in cold water. Cut the kernels from the cobs. Place the fresh or canned corn kernels, eggs, flour, salt, and pepper in a blender and mix together until coarsely chopped. Pour the batter into a small mixing bowl, cover, and set aside.

Slice the goat cheese into ½-ounce rounds. Arrange on a plate; sprinkle with chopped chives, cover, and refrigerate until ready to use.

124   Mostly Vegetables

Cook the watercress in a small saucepan of boiling salted water for 2 minutes. Drain and refresh under cool running water. Press all the moisture from the watercress and pat dry.

In a small saucepan, heat 1 tablespoon of the olive oil over medium-high heat. Add the shallots and sauté until light golden, about 4 minutes. Add the white wine and cook until almost completely reduced and syrupy. Add the water and cream. (You may make the sauce to this point several hours in advance and finish just before serving to keep its color bright green.) Bring the sauce to a simmer and add the watercress leaves. Simmer for 1 minute and puree in a blender. Add the diced tomato and check the seasoning.

Heat a nonstick griddle or large nonstick skillet and then lightly grease it with some of the remaining oil. Add about ½ tablespoon of the corn cake batter. Top with one of the goat cheese rounds. Barely cover the goat cheese with another thin layer of the batter. Cook the corn cake slowly over medium heat for 3 to 4 minutes or until golden on one side; turn and cook until golden brown on the other side. Repeat with the remaining batter, lightly greasing the pan as needed. As the corn cakes are finished, keep them warm in a low oven.

Cover the center of each warm plate with spoonfuls of the watercress sauce. Place 2 corn cakes on each plate and garnish attractively with diced tomato, a few chervil sprigs, and 2 ounces of the smoked salmon slices.

*Buy pale pink salmon that's not too salty. Dark pink salmon often has had smoke salt extract added to turn the fish a darker color—it's unpleasantly smoky.

Mostly Vegetable Main Courses   125

Don't Burn the Onions

The phone rings or something distracts your attention—and you burn the onions, shallots, or garlic for the dish you're preparing. Or maybe you just *begin* to burn them. Start over! Even slightly burned shallots, garlic, or onions will always predominate in a dish, destroying the balance and impact of your other ingredients.

Risotto with Lemon and Herbs

Serves 6

"Waiter, some mullets for Madame and a risotto for me." —Marcel Proust

A lovely risotto for the warmer months, this is best when a blend of 3 or 4 herbs is used. The mint and lemon lift and refresh the starchy rice.

6	cups chicken or vegetable stock, preferably homemade
2	tablespoons minced shallots
3	tablespoons unsalted butter
1	tablespoon olive oil
2	cups Arborio rice
½	cup finely minced fresh herbs such as basil, parsley, rosemary, tarragon, mint, and marjoram
	Zest and juice of 1 lemon
½	cup freshly grated Parmesan cheese
	Salt and freshly ground black pepper to taste

Heat the stock in a saucepan or in the microwave and keep it at a simmer.

In a large saucepan, sauté the shallots in 1 tablespoon of the butter and the oil over medium heat until soft but not browned, about 3 minutes. Add the rice and stir until it is well coated with the oil and begins to become translucent, about 2 minutes.

Add a cup of hot stock, stirring constantly until the rice has absorbed all the liquid. Keep adding stock a cup at a time, stirring all the while and maintaining the heat at a simmer until all the stock is used and the rice is almost tender, about 18 to 20 minutes. Do not cook the rice too fast and try not to let it stick. It should be creamy and al dente.

Remove from the heat and stir in the remaining butter, all the herbs, the lemon zest and lemon juice, and the cheese. Cover and let rest for several minutes to allow the flavors to come together. Season with salt and pepper and serve immediately on warm plates. Decorate with sprigs of herbs or some lemon zest if you wish.

CANTALOUPE WITH

BLACK OLIVES

•

RISOTTO WITH LEMON

AND HERBS

•

JERUSALEM ARTICHOKE,

RADISH, AND

WATERCRESS SALAD

•

CHOCOLATE PUDDING CAKE

WINE SUGGESTIONS:
A CALIFORNIA RIESLING OR A
GERMAN KABINETT MIT
PRÄDIKAT

Risotto—the Art of Making It

Rice that is sautéed in butter with onions and possibly other aromatics, then combined with stock in several additions, stirred constantly, to produce a creamy texture with grains that are still al dente—this is how the Culinary Institute of America defines traditional Italian risotto, a dish that is without a doubt one of the glories of the almost-vegetarian table. Risotto is distinguished more by how it is made than by hard-and-fast rules about what goes into it. It can be basic or complex: redolent of chunky vegetables, wild mushrooms, or seafood; seasoned lightly with saffron and onion, lemon and herbs; or prepared very simply with chicken or vegetable broth, butter, and Parmesan cheese.

Risotto making is an art. It has also acquired a reputation for difficulty since it demands determined stirring for 20 or 30 minutes and must be prepared without pauses at the last minute and served at once. The so-so results achieved from time-saving experiments with microwaving, oven-baking, and pressure-cooking risotto leave me unenthralled. The truth is that the best method is still the old one—cooking on top of the stove. Some things to remember:

- Plump Italian short-grain *superfino* rice is the only rice you should use for risotto. Arborio is the type commonly exported to this country and can be found at some supermarkets, at Italian specialty shops, or through mail-order sources. Two others—Vialone Nano and the expensive Carnaroli (considered by many to be the best of all)—are a lot harder to find. Arborio's fat grains are relatively fast cooking, tender, slightly sticky, decidedly flavorful, with a great capacity to absorb liquids.
- Have all your ingredients on hand before you begin.
- The initial stirring of the rice in butter or oil gives it character and plays a vital role in determining the creamy texture at the end. Don't skip this step.
- Aside from the rice, the broth you use is the single most important element of the dish. It should be richly flavored and not too salty. Make your own, basing it on the principal ingredient you're adding, or select the best you can buy.

Among the supermarket chicken broths, Campbell's Healthy Request Ready-to-Serve Chicken Broth wins the vote of some food critics, but it's worth doing your own taste test.

- Cooks argue about the necessity for constant stirring. If you use a heavy non-stick skillet or saucepan, you might be able to save yourself some labor by waiting until the first addition of water or broth has evaporated and the bottom of the pan is visible before starting to stir. Even better: have a friend on hand from the start to spell you in the stirring.
- Maintain the heat at a gentle simmer.
- Add the vegetables or mushrooms toward the end of the cooking time so that their flavor does not dissipate.
- Partially cooking and then reheating risotto in a skillet with some olive oil makes for an acceptable though not first-rate solution to the problem of last-minute preparation. If you cannot make the entire risotto at the last minute and must work in two stages, stop the risotto about 5 minutes short of completion. Spread the rice on a cold cookie sheet. Once it has reached room temperature, place it in a skillet or the original cooking pot with some melted butter or olive oil, add a final ladleful of the broth, and cook, stirring, until the risotto is done.
- In perfectly cooked risotto, the rice should be slightly chewy but not hard in the center. The creamy sauce should be reduced so that it doesn't separate from the plump grains of rice. The consistency should be almost pourable.

VEGETABLE RISOTTO WITH CARROT, CELERY, AND PARSLEY BROTH

SERVES 6

This is my version of a risotto that chef Michael Romano serves at the Union Square Cafe in New York City. Romano uses a wide array of in-season vegetables in his recipe. If some of these are hard to find, just use more of one you do have or substitute your own favorites.

You need a good juicer to make this.

1	leek, white part only, split in half lengthwise, rinsed well, sliced, paper-thin, and separated into rings
	All-purpose flour for dusting
	Vegetable oil for deep-frying
	Salt and freshly ground black pepper to taste
3	cups fresh celery juice, skimmed, from about 2½ pounds celery
½	cup fresh parsley juice, skimmed, from about 4 bunches of parsley
3	cups fresh carrot juice, skimmed, from about 3 pounds carrots
2	tablespoons olive oil
2	cups Arborio rice
1	teaspoon minced garlic
½	cup dry white wine
½	cup grated carrot, about 1 small carrot
¼	cup green beans in diagonal ½-inch pieces
¼	cup grated zucchini, about 1 small zucchini
½	cup asparagus in ½-inch pieces, about 4 to 6 spears
½	cup quartered artichoke hearts
¼	cup fresh or thawed frozen peas
½	cup finely chopped red bell pepper
2	tablespoons unsalted butter
½	cup freshly grated Parmesan cheese

130 Mostly Vegetables

Lightly dust the leek rings with flour and deep-fry in hot oil for several minutes or until just golden. Drain on absorbent paper, sprinkle with salt, and set aside in a warm place.

Bring the vegetable juices to a simmer in a medium saucepan; skim any solids that rise to the top. Keep warm over low heat.

Heat the olive oil in a large saucepan over medium heat. Add the rice and garlic; stir to coat the rice with oil. Add the wine and stir constantly until it is absorbed.

Add ½ cup of vegetable juice; stir constantly until the liquid is absorbed. Continue adding juice, ½ cup at a time, stirring frequently, until each addition is absorbed, about 20 minutes in all. Stir in the vegetables and cook for 10 minutes longer or until the vegetables are just tender; you may need to add a little water if the rice is not yet creamy and al dente.

Cut the butter into 4 pieces and swirl in one piece at a time. Add the cheese and salt and pepper. Serve immediately, garnishing with the fried leeks.

One recent fall, when the apple trees in our yard bore a crop so generous that it was quite beyond our ability to exploit it (how much applesauce can one family eat?), we found ourselves floundering for solutions to the glut. This was the moment I chose to go out and buy a gleaming stainless-steel Acme Supreme Juicerator 6001, king of the home juicers. In no time the quiet machine had decimated the bumper crop from our trees, turning the apples into a pure juice we then froze and drank through the winter months.

Top-of-the-line juicers are expensive (the Acme is about $300), but they are worth their weight in gold, essential tools for the almost-vegetarian kitchen, turning out fresh fruit juices and broths of aromatic vegetables like fennel, celery, and bell pepper that can be added to vegetables cooked alone or to soups to boost both their taste and their nutritional value. These extractions form the base for a new kind of sauce that neither requires puddles of fat for depth of flavor nor smothers the flavors in the foods they are intended to complement. You can reduce the extracted juices to further concentrate their flavor and color and thicken their texture. You can blend them with oil to create emulsified sauces for drizzling directly onto plates or food.

Technically, these machines are juice extractors, designed to get the juice out of tomatoes, carrots, grapes, apples, celery, peaches, and the like. The principle is simple: food travels from a tube to a cutter disk revolving thousands of times per minute and from there to a strainer, a pulp collector, and a spout from which the juice flows. There are two types: the models with a separate cutter and strainer extract maximum juice; models with a pulp ejector combine cutter and strainer and collect pulp in a separate bin—easier to clean, but not as good at juicing.

Many cooks like the Champion Juicer best, which yields a very thick juice (it's in the Acme price range). Chefs have discovered they can take a whole frozen fruit like a cantaloupe or pear, run it through the Champion, and create instant peak-of-flavor sorbets. The machine grates as well as homogenizes and so lends itself to the grating of vegetables or making of nut butters. However, the Acme is the one to get if what you want is pure pulpless juice. It's also easier to clean than the Champion. In the best of all possible worlds, I would own both.

When shopping for an extractor, keep these points in mind:

- Don't be waylaid by the "citrus juicers." A few extractors do include or sell separately an attachment to juice citrus fruit. Consider a citrus juicer only if all you want is some fresh orange juice in the morning.
- The wider the feed tube of your juicer, the less time you will spend cutting food into small chunks.
- Look for a juicer that lets you see how much pulp has accumulated.
- Models with a detachable one-piece top are easiest to clean.

If you plan to use your juicer a lot, consider one of the more expensive models. In the long run the machine will pay for itself. If you plan to juice only occasionally, the best of the less expensive models will serve you reliably and well.

Risotto with Sweet Corn

This recipe comes from Julie Anne Wagner, one of the truly gifted cooks and hostesses in the Napa Valley. Her risotto, full-flavored and forthright, is just what you want along with the Catahoula's Tomatoes-in-All-Their-Glory Salad on evenings when sweet corn is in season. As much as I look forward to fresh-picked corn on the cob in the summer, this is more satisfying and more grown-up.

6	ears corn
1	quart chicken stock, preferably homemade
2	tablespoons olive oil
4	tablespoons unsalted butter
½	cup finely chopped yellow onion
1	cup Arborio rice
½	cup freshly grated Parmesan cheese
	Salt and freshly ground black pepper to taste
2	tablespoons minced fresh sage leaves for garnish

Using a small sharp knife, cut the corn kernels off the cobs. Reserve 1 cup of the kernels and set aside. In a food processor or blender, blend the remaining kernels with 1 cup of the stock until liquefied. Strain through a sieve; you should have about 2 cups corn milk.

Place the remaining stock in a saucepan and bring to a bare simmer. Add the corn milk. Keep at a slow simmer.

In a heavy flameproof casserole or skillet, heat the olive oil and 2 tablespoons of the butter over medium heat. Add the onion and sauté until translucent, about 4 minutes.

Add the rice, stirring to coat thoroughly with the butter and oil. Add ½ cup of the simmering stock, stirring constantly with a wooden spoon. When all the liquid has been absorbed, add another ½ cup. Continue this process, stirring constantly, until all the stock has been added and absorbed, about 20 minutes in all.

When the rice is tender but still slightly firm to the bite, add the reserved corn kernels, the remaining 2 tablespoons butter, and the Parmesan. Mix thoroughly. Season with salt and pepper, decorate with sage, and serve at once.

Vegetarian Cassoulet

SERVES 6

Wanting to eat less meat and fat doesn't mean you have to give up some of your favorite dishes. I have found that signature spices juxtaposed with the right combination of ingredients will often satisfy my craving for a certain food I feel I cannot do without. Here the combination of the traditional *quatre épices* seasonings (a traditional spice mixture of France), bread crumbs, garlic, and beans still reads "cassoulet" to me without all the meat and preserved duck. The Golden Veal Stock greatly enhances the taste of this dish. I don't serve bread with this because it's filling enough on its own.

2	cups dried Great Northern beans, picked over
1	tablespoon *quatre épices* (recipe follows)
3	garlic cloves, minced, plus 1 head of garlic, peeled
2	tablespoons salt
18	pearl onions
2½	cups veal or chicken stock, preferably homemade
12	baby carrots
1	bunch of Swiss chard, ribs removed, leaves rinsed and chopped
	Oil for the dish
¼	cup fresh bread crumbs
¼	cup olive oil or melted unsalted butter

Soak the beans in cold water to cover for 4 to 6 hours or overnight, drain, and put in a large saucepan with the *quatre épices,* minced garlic, and salt. Bring to a simmer and cook, uncovered, for 1 hour or until just tender.

To make onion peeling easy, drop them into boiling water for about 10 seconds; transfer to a bowl of ice water with a slotted spoon. Peel the onions and cut a cross ¼ inch deep in their root ends to keep them from bursting when cooked.

While the beans are cooking, place the peeled onions in a large saucepan with the stock. Simmer, uncovered, for 15 minutes. Add ½ cup of the bean

SUN-DRIED TOMATO AND
GRUYÈRE CHEESE PUFFS

•

VEGETARIAN CASSOULET

•

MUSHROOM SALAD

•

TUSCAN FIG AND
BREAD TART

WINE SUGGESTIONS:
A MEDIUM-BODIED CALIFORNIA
ZINFANDEL OR A CHIANTI
CLASSICO RISERVA

liquid to the broth and cook for 15 minutes more or until the onions are just tender. Remove with a slotted spoon to a platter.

Cook the carrots in the same broth for 10 to 15 minutes or until barely tender. Remove with a slotted spoon to a platter.

Next add the Swiss chard to the broth and simmer, uncovered, for 5 minutes. Remove to a platter with a slotted spoon.

Preheat the oven to 325°F.

To assemble the cassoulet, oil a 4- to 5-quart casserole dish. Add the cooked beans and the broth in which you have cooked the vegetables. Add the cooked vegetables and peeled garlic cloves, tucking them into the beans. Sprinkle the bread crumbs on top and drizzle with the oil. Bake for 1½ hours or until the crust is golden, the broth evaporated, and the beans enveloped in a thick, creamy sauce.

Quatre Épices

MAKES ABOUT ⅓ CUP

Quatre épices means literally "4 spices." There's really no set-in-stone formula for it and, though this version has more than 4 spices, it's my current favorite. *Quatre épices* is one of the secrets of great French pâtés and cassoulets.

1	teaspoon ground cumin
1	teaspoon ground coriander
1	teaspoon ground cinnamon
¾	teaspoon ground allspice
¼	teaspoon ground cloves
½	teaspoon ground cardamom
½	teaspoon ground ginger
½	teaspoon grated nutmeg
1	bay leaf, crumbled
¾	teaspoon dried thyme

Mix the spices and dried herbs together in a blender until you have a fine powder. Store in a small jar with a tight-fitting lid.

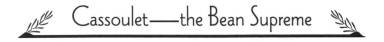

Cassoulet—the Bean Supreme

"Cassoulet, like life itself, is not so simple as it seems." —Paula Wolfert

A succulent casserole of meats and dried beans, cassoulet is one of those extraordinary dishes that, in the hands of a gifted cook, greatly exceeds the sum of its parts. Probably because it is so receptive to inspiration, there is a mystique about it and no absolutely right way of going about its preparation. It is one of several great regional specialties contributed to gastronomy by the charmed southwestern corner of France, the particulars of each recipe changing from Toulouse, to Carcassonne, to Castelnaudary.

Much more than just a good meal of baked beans, classic cassoulet is replete with as many as five kinds of meat as well as a battery of stocks, sauces, and herbs. It is labor-intensive and long-simmering. Anatole France is believed to have especially enjoyed a mellow cassoulet that tasted, in his estimation, as if it had been cooking for twenty years. Modern adaptations tend to downplay the great stew's more opulent ingredients such as confit of goose, fresh pork skin, and quartered ducks, paring down the mix so it's not so stuffing and fatty; these recipes employ reduced quantities of sausage, pork, or lamb mainly as flavor garnishes. The low-fat Vegetarian Cassoulet goes even further, drawing its meat flavor exclusively from stock and leaving center stage to a traditional combination of rustic vegetables in a garlic- and herb-suffused sauce—very fragrant, very filling.

I know of no better description of the intrigue and excitement surrounding the making of authentic cassoulet than Paula Wolfert's in her wonderful book *The Cooking of South-West France* (Dial Press, 1983). Paula went to all the great cassoulet towns and found her favorite rendering in Auch at the hand of Gascon chef André Daguin. It was prepared with fresh fava beans, the original bean used to make cassoulet before the now traditional white bean was cultivated in France.

Wild Mushroom Bread Pudding

An American classic reinterpreted.

Dried mushrooms give lots of flavor per ounce and are less expensive and more readily available than fresh wild mushrooms. The soaking broth from the reconstituted mushrooms provides rich, musky mushroom flavor when added to the pudding or made into a sauce.

¾ ounce dried shiitake mushrooms, stemmed
4   ounces dried chanterelles, stems removed
2   cups warm water
4   cups bread in ¾-inch cubes, preferably a hearty/levain-
    type loaf
5   large eggs, beaten
    Salt and freshly ground black pepper to taste
2½ to 3 cups milk or half-and-half
1   cup dry white wine
½   cup plus 1 tablespoon minced shallots
2   parsley stems
1   pound white mushrooms, stemmed and sliced
7   tablespoons unsalted butter plus butter for the baking
    dish
1   teaspoon minced garlic
½   cup minced fresh herbs such as thyme, parsley, sage,
    chives, and marjoram
½   pound Italian Fontina cheese, coarsely grated
¼   cup freshly grated Parmesan cheese
1 to 2 teaspoons fresh lemon juice

Soak the dried mushrooms in the warm water for at least 30 minutes. Strain the mushroom liquid through a strainer lined with several layers of rinsed cheesecloth and set aside. Rinse the reconstituted mushrooms and pat dry.

Place the bread cubes in a single layer in a shallow dish. Combine the

Wine suggestions:
A fruity red Côtes-du-Rhône or a California Zinfandel. If you are serving this around Thanksgiving try a newly released Beaujolais nouveau.

eggs, ½ teaspoon salt, and the milk. Pour over the bread and let sit for about 30 minutes.

While the bread cubes are soaking, combine the wine, shallots, and parsley stems in a small saucepan over high heat and reduce to ½ cup. Strain; discard the vegetables.

In a large skillet, sauté the white mushrooms in 2 tablespoons of the butter over medium heat until they just begin to wilt, about 3 minutes; add the reconstituted mushrooms and garlic; cook for 1 minute, then add the reduced wine. Cook until all the liquid has disappeared. Toss with the herbs.

Preheat the oven to 325°F. Butter a 3-quart baking dish.

Press the bread cubes to extract the milk-egg mixture. Set the liquid aside.

Layer a third of the bread in the prepared dish. Place half of the mushroom mixture on top of the bread. Strew a third of each of the cheeses over the mushrooms. Repeat the layering, using half of the remaining bread, all of the remaining mushrooms, and half of the remaining cheese. Arrange the remaining bread on top and strew the remaining cheese over it. Pour the milk-egg mixture over the layers and dot with 1 tablespoon of butter cut into small pieces.

Bake for about 45 minutes or until the egg mixture is set. If the top browns too quickly, cover it with an aluminum foil tent.

To make the sauce, over high heat reduce the mushroom-soaking liquid to 1 cup, whisk in the remaining 4 tablespoons butter, and correct the seasoning with lemon juice and salt and pepper.

To serve, spoon some of the reduced mushroom sauce over large spoonfuls of the bread pudding.

Bread Pudding—
Turning the Sweet to Savory

Surely one of the great custard desserts, bread pudding has come a long way since the days when frugal countrywomen turned to it to use up stale bread. Shifted from its traditional position, bread pudding becomes a marvelous main event, its smooth custard providing a rich background for the flavors of smoky mushrooms or winter root crops. Add bread pudding to a Thanksgiving feast and it becomes the supreme replacement for stuffing. Just by itself it is lavish feasting food.

Choose vegetable combinations with care and you will be surprised with the elegance of the result. Bread puddings are obliging and simple to make but cannot soar unless the ingredients are first-rate. Use good bread with some real texture; the better the bread, the better the pudding.

Mushroom Primer

There are two things my husband and I have agreed not to talk about with other people: the details of our private life and where the chanterelles grow in the fall along the road to Sonoma. Anyone who has ever hunted mushrooms in the wild understands the thrill of finding a colony of a choice edible species, and avid collectors everywhere guard their secret caches as jealously as fishermen their lucky fishing holes. A harvest of a rare wild mushroom is a treasure to be, well, guarded.

In the kitchen, mushrooms manage to be simultaneously meaty and light and *haut*. Too often relegated to use as a garnish or as a bit player in classic beef and poultry stews, mushrooms when moved front and center provide a great window of opportunity for the almost-vegetarian cook. They suggest meat. Their substance and complex smoky savor are remarkable and various when used as the basis for pasta dishes, stir-fries, warm salads, or simple but elegant grain dishes. The best of them absorb flavors while surrendering none of their own. Drying mushrooms concentrates their full flavor, and when dried mushrooms are rehydrated the resulting broth adds depth of flavor to many soups and sauces, as satisfying as beef stock.

SELECTION AND STORAGE. Choose fresh mushrooms that are firm, unblemished, and dry but not desiccated. Avoid limp, discolored, or slimy-looking specimens with any "off" smell. Store in the refrigerator unwashed in an open box, bowl, paper bag, or the original packaging. Depending on variety, they will keep for up to five days.

CLEANING. Don't clean mushrooms until you're ready to cook them. Mushrooms lose their flavor when soaked in water. The alternative method of wiping them with a clean, damp towel is effective for cultivated mushrooms bought at a market. However, for those gathered from the wild and covered with debris, a clean towel or mushroom brush is simply not up to the job. Although some flavor will be sacrificed, you can rid the wild specimens of unwanted litter or insects or worms by submerging them quickly in successive bowls of cold water; drain and pat dry. Never subject mushrooms to a stream of hot or cold running water; the pressure of the stream is too much for these delicate specimens, and the extended exposure to water will make them soggy.

HANDLING. Don't peel mushrooms. There's no need, and you'll lose flavor and nutrients. Try cooking several varieties in combination to produce flavors of intriguing complexity. To reconstitute dried mushrooms, rinse in cold water and soak in hot water for at least 30 minutes in a nonmetal container. Add the drained liquid to soups or use for cooking grains and vegetables. To make a richer extract, reduce over low heat by half or more, depending on the potency desired. Mushroom extracts can be refrigerated for up to a week or kept frozen without loss of character for several months.

SOURCES. You can mail-order fresh and dried exotic mushrooms from Fresh and Wild, Inc., P.O. Box 2981, Vancouver, WA 98668 (800-222-5578), and French and Italian dried mushrooms from Dean & Deluca, Inc., Mail Order Department, 560 Broadway, New York, NY 10012 (800-221-7714). Or you might try growing your own certified-organic gourmet mushrooms at home by ordering a guaranteed-to-produce kit from Fungi Perfecti, P.O. Box 7634, Olympia, WA 98507 (206-426-9292).

The Cultivated

COMMON BUTTON: Young or "button" form of the common market mushroom *Agaricus bisporus,* often sold mature with cap opened, showing dark brown gills. Raw, they lack aroma and flavor (Colette hated them!), but cooked they have a mild "mushroomy" taste and absorb well the flavors of other varieties.

Sauté in a hot pan in butter until juice is released and evaporated and caps turn golden in color; classic in *duxelles* or *à la Grecque* preparations.

CREMINI: Light brown version of the common button mushroom; more flavorful than the white button; increasingly available in supermarkets.

Prepare as you would the button mushroom; turns dark brown when sautéed in butter; good flavor.

ENOKI (ENOKIDAKE): Tiny, with white caps and long trailing stems; slightly crunchy; flavor not earthy but fruity and slightly acid, more like a grape than a mushroom; available fresh, usually in plastic packages, in Asian groceries and some super-markets.

Sprinkle raw on dishes featuring other mushrooms; great as a garnish for salads with Asian flavors.

SHIITAKE (CHINESE BLACK MUSHROOM, BLACK FOREST MUSHROOM): Most widely used mushroom in Asian cooking; dark brown to gold saucer-shaped caps with tough, fibrous stems; intense flavor and aroma when dried; milder with distinct garlic-piney-smoky aroma and lush, supple texture when fresh; sold fresh in many markets and dried in health food and Asian stores.

Grill, sauté, or add to stir-fries and clear soups.

PORTOBELLO: The "prime rib" of the mushroom kingdom; enormous (as much as 10 inches in diameter), brown to taupe, thick, slightly shaggy caps with tough stems; milder taste than porcino but meaty and rich; widely available. One grilled cap makes a meal.

Stuff whole caps; grill and serve on toast or in a sandwich; combine with other mushrooms, vegetables, and meat.

The Wild

CHANTERELLE (GIROLLE): Vase-shaped with a frilled edge, veinlike gills, and fleshy stem; egg yolk to apricot colored; mild, delicate flavor reminiscent of apricots, but varying from flowery to nutty to softly spicy depending on location; not cultivated commercially.

Sauté and toss with pasta; add to broth for sauces and soups; good with seafood, poultry, and meats; add to garden ragouts, gratins, risotto; braise and toss small-sized mushrooms in salads.

MOREL (MORILLE, MORCHELLA): Brown to off-white, easily recognized by its spongy honeycombed cap; magnificent woodsy taste suggestive of hazelnuts; available fresh early spring through July; dried, year-round; not cultivated.

Add to sauces with other vegetables; sauté by itself or with other vegetables, especially asparagus; good with meat or poultry; gratins, risotto, ragouts.

HORN OF PLENTY (CRATERELLE, BLACK TRUMPET, TROMPETTE-DE-LA-MORT): Trumpet-shaped with veinlike gills and frilled edge, nearly black on top, gray beneath, with ash-gray to black tubular stem; called "poor man's truffle" for its texture and pungent aroma; deep, nutty, slightly astringent flavor; available fresh summer and fall; not cultivated.

Risotto, gratins; assertive flavor stands up to meats and poultry.

PORCINO—PL., PORCINI (CÈPE, BOLETE): Widely eaten in Europe; large buff or dark brown caps, with numerous vertical tubes on the underside instead of gills, thick bulbous stems; robust smoky flavor; fresh, has pale, pungent, firm, and meaty flesh; available fresh in spring and fall in very limited supply; sold dried in Italian stores, gourmet stores, and some supermarkets. (Note: South American imports are cheaper.)

Sauté; grill; combine with other mushrooms, vegetables, and meat; make a broth or add to soups, stews, pasta sauces, pilafs, risotto, gratins, and sauces for other vegetables.

OYSTER (PLEUROTTE, SHIMEJI): Smooth, silvery-taupe fan-shaped caps with deep gills, often in clumps; fragrant; mild, buttery flavor reminiscent of oysters; meltingly silky texture.

Sauté by itself with garlic and herbs or with other mushrooms; sauté and toss with pasta; grill.

HEN-OF-THE-WOODS: Curious-looking gray, black, and white mushroom, bushy in form, somewhat resembling a brain, 3 to 5 inches in diameter; tender, with smoky-sweet flavor; hard to find, but available hothouse year-round.

Star in a gratin with cream, bread crumbs, garlic, and parsley.

FARCI WITH FRESH WHITE CHEESE
(FARCI AU FROMAGE BLANC)

SERVES 8 TO 10

If the potato is king of comfort foods, then this hearty *farci* is perhaps the most comforting dish ever set before mortal man. Very rich, very satisfying. Just the thing for a cold winter's evening after a great day of skiing in bright, tingling mountain air. The ancient preparations called *farci, farcement,* or *farcon* depending on a rather long list of local variables are probably *the* signature dishes of the Savoie in the French Alps.

These sturdy regional specialties have evolved over hundreds of years (the oldest versions containing no potatoes at all), and there are literally dozens of recipes for them, but in its modern form the basic dish can be described as a pudding of potatoes pureed or grated and combined with eggs and milk or cream and slow-cooked in the oven or in a *bain-marie* (water bath). Cabbage, bacon, herbs, and fresh or dried fruit are frequent additions.

This *farci* is an adaptation of a recipe idea of the incomparable Madeleine Kamman, who communicates a passionate love for the Savoie, where she spent many summers of her childhood. It takes a while to prepare and bake but is well worth the time and effort. Very filling, it needs to be accompanied only by a nice crisp salad such as the Parsley and Mint Salad.

12	**large outer leaves of Savoy or Napa cabbage**
2	**pounds Yukon Gold potatoes**
1	**cup heavy cream**
¼	**teaspoon grated nutmeg**
1	**pound creamed cottage cheese**
¼	**pound cream cheese, whipped**
6	**large eggs, well beaten**
⅔	**cup fresh rye bread crumbs**
	Salt and freshly ground black pepper
½	**cup unsalted butter, melted**
2	**tablespoons cold unsalted butter**

ESCAROLE-SHALLOT-APPLE

TARTE TATIN

•

FARCI WITH FRESH

WHITE CHEESE

•

PARSLEY AND MINT SALAD

•

CARROTS WITH ANISEED

•

FRESH FRUIT WITH

GOOD SPIRITS

•

LAVENDER SHORTBREADS

WINE SUGGESTIONS:
A FRESH WHITE WINE FROM
HAUTE-SAVOIE OR AN
OREGON PINOT GRIS

Preheat the oven to 300°F.

Drop the cabbage leaves briefly into a large pot of boiling water; drain and dry them. In the same pot, boil the potatoes in their skins. Meanwhile, scald the cream in a large saucepan and add the nutmeg. As soon as the potatoes are cooked, skin them, then rice them or push them quickly through a mesh strainer into the cream. Add the cheeses, eggs, bread crumbs, salt, pepper, and ¼ cup of the melted butter. Mix thoroughly.

Butter a heavy 5-quart baking dish with the cold butter. Remove the ribs of the blanched cabbage leaves and discard. Line the bottom and sides of the baking dish with the cabbage leaves, overlapping the leaves slightly. Distribute the potato-cheese mixture over the cabbage. Pour the rest of the melted butter on top. Cover first with a layer of plastic wrap, then with heavy-duty foil.

Bake for 2½ to 3 hours. Cool slightly before serving. To serve, either slice like cheesecake or spoon it onto plates.

GRILLED TUNA WITH SAFFRON VINAIGRETTE

This warm salad is good in summer or winter as a luncheon dish or first course. Don't overcook the tuna.

1½ pounds fresh tuna steak, cut ½ to ¾ inch thick
1   medium leek, split in half lengthwise, rinsed well, and
       cut into ½-inch pieces
2   shallots, thinly sliced
1   red onion, cut in half crosswise, then cut lengthwise
       into thin strips
1   teaspoon finely chopped fresh thyme
1   cup plus 1 tablespoon olive oil
2   healthy pinches of saffron threads, plus a little for
       garnish, optional
5   medium Idaho potatoes, peeled and cut into ½-inch
       cubes
1   teaspoon Dijon mustard
½   cup white wine vinegar
    Salt and freshly ground black pepper to taste
5   medium ripe tomatoes, seeded and coarsely chopped
6   cups small-leafed lettuces

Preheat a grill to medium-high heat. Brush it well with oil to prevent the tuna from sticking.

In a medium skillet, combine the leek, shallots, onion, thyme, and 1 tablespoon of the olive oil. Cover with wax paper and then with a tight-fitting lid and cook the mixture over very low heat for 15 to 20 minutes or until very soft. Set aside.

In a small saucepan, warm the remaining olive oil with the saffron threads and set aside for 20 minutes.

Meanwhile, boil the potatoes in lightly salted water until tender, about 5 minutes. Drain.

Prepare the vinaigrette by mixing together the mustard and vinegar, then blending in the saffron oil. Season with salt and pepper.

SHREDDED ZUCCHINI SALAD

•

GRILLED TUNA WITH SAFFRON

VINAIGRETTE

•

GOAT CHEESE CAKE AND SALAD

OF MIXED GREENS

•

FRESH FRUIT WITH

GOOD SPIRITS

•

LAVENDER SHORTBREADS

WINE SUGGESTIONS:
A FRENCH POUILLY-FUMÉ OR A
MEDIUM-BODIED CALIFORNIA
SAUVIGNON BLANC

Grill the tuna for about 2 minutes on each side or to desired doneness.

In a bowl, toss together the potatoes and tomatoes; dress with ¾ cup of the vinaigrette. Arrange the lettuce on individual serving plates, mound some of the potato-tomato salad in the center, top with portions of grilled tuna, then add some of the onion mixture. Drizzle some of the remaining vinaigrette over each serving and, if you wish, top with a sprinkle of saffron threads. Serve at once.

HUBERT KELLER'S SUCCULENT TRUFFLED POTATO STEW WITH PÂTÉ À L'EAU

SERVES 6

A sublime potato dish from the brilliant chef and restaurateur. Hubert's genius with vegetables is unrivaled, and in this robust and delicious preparation he elevates the humble spud to new heights of luxuriance—without adding a trace of fat! Traditionally, in France where it originated, the stew included fat and lots of it—beef, pork, lamb, and pigs' feet were tossed into the casserole. Hubert's rendering gains its succulent character by other means: "Truffles are not, of course, a vegetable," he will tell you. "They are a miracle." He's right, but they are hardly an inexpensive miracle, so I usually use fresh or dried mushrooms in their place and drizzle just a little truffle oil over each portion before serving.

The *pâté à l'eau* used for luting, or hermetically sealing, the casserole is a very simple pastry made by mixing flour with enough water to form a soft paste. Brought to the table with its ribbons of pastry still intact, the casserole makes a dramatic presentation at a casual dinner party. Break the seal as you serve the stew.

3	pounds firm potatoes, peeled and sliced into thin rounds
2	garlic cloves, finely chopped
1	onion, finely diced
¼	cup coarsely chopped carrot
¼	cup coarsely chopped celery
1	small leek, white part only, split in half lengthwise, rinsed well, and finely julienned
1	fresh thyme sprig
1½	ounces fresh truffles (or ¾ ounce dried shiitakes, morels, or chanterelles soaked to rehydrate), julienned
	Salt and freshly ground black pepper to taste
	Oil or butter for the tureen
1	cup dry white wine

PHYLLO STRUDEL WITH FETA,
SUN-DRIED TOMATOES,
AND OLIVES

•

HUBERT KELLER'S SUCCULENT
TRUFFLED POTATO STEW WITH
PÂTÉ À L'EAU

•

WARM BEET SALAD WITH
WALNUTS AND DILL

•

PERFECT GINGERBREAD

WINE SUGGESTIONS:
AN ITALIAN DOLCETTO OR A
MEDIUM-BODIED
DRY CREEK ZINFANDEL

Pastry

¾   **cup all-purpose flour**
5   **tablespoons cold water**
1   **tablespoon oil**

Preheat the oven to 350°F.

In a large mixing bowl, combine the potatoes, garlic, onion, carrot, celery, leek, thyme, and truffles. Season with salt and pepper and toss gently.

Lightly grease a large ovenproof earthenware tureen or casserole with a lid. Transfer the vegetable mixture to the casserole. Pour on the white wine and enough water to barely cover the vegetables. (If you're using dried mushrooms, use the strained water in which they were rehydrated as part of or in place of the water.) Seal with a simple dough made from the flour, water, and oil: Roll the dough into a rope about 28 inches long and 2 inches wide and wrap it around the seam between the casserole cover and the casserole; pinch the ends together and seal with a drop or two of water if necessary. Cover the casserole and bake for 1 hour; a little longer won't hurt.

Unearthing the Rare Truffle

Plan on using fresh truffles at the right time of year—this is a seasonal "crop." Fresh black truffles are available by mail order from November through February from Delices des Bois (4 Leonard St., New York, NY 10012; 212-334-1230) at about $35 to $50 an ounce. Fresh white truffles are available from September through January from Urbani Truffle (29-24 40th Avenue, Long Island City, NY 11101; 718-392-5050) at about $85 an ounce. Both truffles may be found in choice markets for the year-end holidays. If you can't afford the fresh article, top-quality preserved truffles sold in glass jars are a good second choice since you can see what you are buying. The tinned truffles, truffle peelings, and truffle pieces often stocked in gourmet shops are disappointing substitutes.

Good truffle oils are increasingly available in upscale markets and through mail-order sources. These work wonders sprinkled on risotto, pasta, polenta, mushrooms, sturdy bread, and mashed potatoes. Agribusco white truffle oil, at about $15 for 3½ ounces, can be ordered from Zingerman's Delicatessen (422 Detroit St., Ann Arbor, MI 48104; 313-769-1625). Or make your own truffle oil by following these simple directions: in a small bottle, steep at least ¼ ounce of carefully cleaned fresh white truffles in a cup of extra-virgin olive oil for three to four days. Use sparingly.

GRATIN OF POTATOES AND FENNEL WITH ROUILLE

SERVES 6 TO 8

Rust-colored *rouille*, the pungent red pepper and garlic mayonnaise from Provence, enlivens this vegetable gratin. Saffron turns it a lovely gold. You can roast the fennel and the red pepper, and make the *rouille* a day ahead of time.

WINE SUGGESTIONS:
A GIGONDAS OR A MEDIUM-
BODIED CALIFORNIA
RHÔNE BLEND

	Oil or butter for the gratin dish
2	large fennel bulbs, trimmed and cored
2	red bell peppers, roasted, peeled, and seeded
1	cup fresh bread crumbs
¼	teaspoon saffron threads dissolved in 3 tablespoons hot water
	Generous pinch of cayenne pepper
4	garlic cloves, peeled
3	large egg yolks
1½	cups olive oil
	Fresh lemon juice and salt to taste
6	medium potatoes, peeled and sliced ⅛ inch thick

Preheat the oven to 350°F. Lightly grease an 8-cup gratin or baking dish.

Wrap the fennel bulbs tightly in foil and bake for 1½ hours.

To prepare the *rouille*, in a food processor combine the roasted red peppers, bread crumbs, dissolved saffron, cayenne, garlic, egg yolks, and any juice from the roasted fennel bulbs and process until well blended. With the motor running, add the olive oil in a thin stream and blend until it is all incorporated. Season with lemon juice and salt.

Put the potatoes in a saucepan with salted water to cover. Bring to a simmer and cook for 3 to 5 minutes or until barely tender. Slice the fennel. Drain the potatoes and cool for a few minutes. Gently combine the potatoes, fennel, and *rouille* and spoon into the prepared gratin dish; smooth the surface. Increase the oven temperature to 400°F and bake for about 20 minutes or until the top is golden and crusty. Serve at once.

Eggplant Torte with Fresh Tomato Compote

SERVES 6 AS A MAIN COURSE

This distinctive dish was inspired by a recipe of inimitable French chef Roger Vergé in his *Roger Vergé's Vegetables in the French Style* (Artisan, 1994). Build a dinner around this dish or serve smaller slices as a first course. The tomato compote is good on just about anything—from toasted bruschetta to pasta, grilled fish or chicken.

	Oil for the pan
3	medium eggplants
5	tablespoons olive oil
1	medium onion, chopped
3	garlic cloves
½	cup fresh or dried unseasoned bread crumbs
2	large eggs, lightly beaten
1	teaspoon Chinese five-spice powder
¼	teaspoon Tabasco sauce
¾	cup heavy cream
½	teaspoon salt
	Freshly ground black pepper to taste
1	red bell pepper, roasted, peeled, seeded, and chopped
	Fresh Tomato Compote (recipe follows)

GRILLED VINE LEAF PARCELS

•

EGGPLANT TORTE WITH FRESH TOMATO COMPOTE

•

SAVORY BAKED RICOTTA

•

ZUCCHINI CAKE WITH FRUIT AND NUTS

WINE SUGGESTIONS:
A SIMPLE COTEAUX DU LANGUEDOC OR A LIGHTER-BODIED CALIFORNIA CABERNET SAUVIGNON

Preheat the oven to 375°F. Oil an 8-inch springform pan.

Trim and halve the eggplants lengthwise. Sprinkle with 4 tablespoons (¼ cup) of the olive oil. Place on a baking sheet cut side up and bake for 40 to 45 minutes or until the flesh is quite soft. Cool.

Reduce the oven temperature to 325°F.

In a skillet over medium heat, cook the onion and garlic in the remaining oil until tender but not brown, about 3 minutes.

Scrape out the flesh of the eggplants, taking care not to tear the skins. Coarsely chop the flesh, pressing and straining out any bitter juices. Cut the eggplant skins lengthwise into long 1-inch-wide strips. Line the bottom and sides of the prepared pan with the strips, shiny side down, overlapping them slightly. Sprinkle the bread crumbs over the eggplant strips and shake well so the entire surface is well coated.

In a medium bowl, blend the eggs, five-spice powder, Tabasco, and cream. Season with salt and pepper. Fold in the eggplant, onion, garlic, and red pepper. Pour into the prepared pan, cover with aluminum foil, and bake for 30 to 35 minutes. Cool for 15 minutes, then unmold onto a serving platter. Cool for 1 hour before slicing.

To serve, top each slice with several tablespoons of Fresh Tomato Compote.

Fresh Tomato Compote

MAKES ABOUT 3 CUPS

1   pound ripe high-acid tomatoes, coarsely chopped, about 1½ cups
¾   cup loosely packed julienned basil leaves (anise or Thai basil would be great)
1   teaspoon finely minced garlic
3   tablespoons extra-virgin olive oil
1   tablespoon balsamic vinegar or fresh lemon juice, optional
1 to 2 teaspoons salt

Thoroughly combine all ingredients in a mixing bowl. Allow to sit at room temperature for 1 hour before serving.

Salting the Eggplant

Glossy and gorgeous though it may be, eggplant has a reputation for bitterness. It contains a chemical called *solanine,* which, depending on the type of eggplant used and its preparation, can cause the flesh of the vegetable to taste bitter. To counter this tendency when grilling or frying eggplant (the two cooking methods that concentrate the bitter component), sprinkle coarse salt on the cut eggplant, drain it in a colander for 30 minutes to an hour, brush off the salt with a damp cloth, press to squeeze out the moisture, and pat dry. Adjust the seasoning of your recipe to compensate for the added salt. (By reducing the eggplant's moisture content, salting also makes the texture denser, reducing the amount of oil needed to fry it.) In dishes that call for long simmering or pureeing, bitterness should not be a problem.

Another neat trick to release most of the bitterness: first, place slices on a tray in the freezer. Remove them after 4 hours and, when thawed, press out the excess moisture.

The bitter property tends to be most pronounced in the midnight-purple fully mature, often seedy European-type eggplant found in supermarkets. When shopping for these, select firm, medium-size specimens. Long lavender-to-purple Japanese eggplant is not bitter. Meltingly tender, with flesh that has few seeds, it holds its shape in baking and is a good choice for sautéing, steaming, or stir-frying. On the other hand, the small round Thai eggplants are actually prized for their bitter flavor. These tart midgets are best appreciated pickled or added raw to soups and sauces.

Speedy Pasta Meals from Simple Sauces

I make these quick sauces for last-minute meals or anytime I feel the need for a no-brainer dinner—occasions that arise frequently for all of us. Robust basil-scented pesto has been the standard quick-fix pasta sauce for years, but fortunately we are moving on, switching to other aromatic combinations with flavors just as vigorous. The sauces in this section are some of my favorites. Perhaps at least one of them will make its way into your battery of emergency meals-in-a-moment.

A few tips on success with these fresh-tasting sauces:

• Stock your pantry and refrigerator with ingredients you like with your pasta. Here's a partial list of raw materials you might want to keep on hand:

From the Pantry:
canned artichoke hearts
canned Italian tuna
canned anchovies
canned Italian plum tomatoes
sun-dried tomatoes
tapenade, green or black or a combination
walnuts
pine nuts
pistachios
capers
imported olives such as Gaeta, Nyons, Kalamata
seasoned oils
balsamic vinegar
dried mushrooms (porcini, shiitake, chanterelles)
cannellini, Great Northern, or navy beans
golden raisins

From the Refrigerator:
cheese: Parmesan, Asiago, Fontina, Gorgonzola, Romano, mozzarella,
and feta

pancetta (freezer)
peas (freezer)

For your fresh ingredients, in-season bumper crops should provide many ideas. Garden- or container-grown fresh herbs such as flat-leaf parsley, thyme, basil, oregano, and rosemary are of inestimable value. Remember: the better the quality of your ingredients, the less you need to do to them.

- Choose your vegetable combinations carefully. Two or three compatible ingredients add up to more than a mish-mash of conflicting flavors.
- Heighten flavor by caramelizing your onions and shallots or roasting vegetables in a hot oven before adding them to your sauce.
- Freshen up flavor at the last minute by sprinkling on a little of one of the new flavored oils or tossing some chopped fresh herbs with your pasta. Gremolata—the savory Italian blend of lemon zest, minced garlic, and chopped parsley—is a specially enlivening garnish.
- Use any pasta shape you are partial to at the moment. It's true that some shapes work best with certain kinds of sauces, but even as I am moved by fashions in clothes, with dried pastas I go from shape to fanciful shape for no particular reason. Some shapes to seek out: orecchiette ("little ears"); farfalle ("butterflies"); penne ("quills"); tagliatelle (a ribbon-type pasta similar to fettuccine); and capellini (very fine spaghetti strands).
- Treat yourself now and then to fresh pasta for the more delicate sauces. It cooks in minutes and has a silky, tender-to-the-bite texture unlike the al dente quality of dried pasta. I could never recommend that you make your own, mainly because I don't. And don't feel guilty: They don't in Italy either, for the same reason. It's too easy to find a good local source, either the supermarket (check the freshness date on the package) or a specialty food shop.

Each of these recipes makes enough sauce for 1 pound of cooked pasta. Read through each recipe before you begin—several require that you save some of the pasta cooking water.

Artichoke Hearts Picante

Makes 1 cup

This intensely flavored quick Italian sauce from Noodles in St. Helena, California, is easy to make and terrific over pasta. Keep the ingredients on hand in your pantry for last-minute meals and unexpected guests. Low in fat, the sauce gets its creamy texture from pureed hearts of artichoke.

- 2 **garlic cloves**
- 1 **teaspoon hot red pepper flakes**
- 1 **teaspoon fresh oregano leaves**
- 2 **tablespoons olive oil**
- 1 **12-ounce can artichoke hearts packed in water, drained**
- 1 **12-ounce jar roasted red bell peppers**
- 2 **teaspoons drained capers**
  Salt and freshly ground black pepper to taste

In a skillet over medium heat, sauté the garlic, red pepper flakes, and oregano in the olive oil until the garlic is soft but not browned, about 1 minute. Add the artichoke hearts and roasted peppers. Simmer for about 10 minutes. Cool.

Puree the mixture in a blender or food processor. Fold in the capers and season with salt and pepper.

Pasta Sauce with Cauliflower, Anchovies, Garlic, and Hot Red Pepper Flakes

Cook 1 large head of cauliflower in boiling salted water until tender, about 20 minutes. Drain well. Gently cook 2 large garlic cloves, minced, and 4 to 6 rinsed and chopped anchovy fillets in ¼ cup olive oil in a deep 12-inch sauté pan over medium heat until the garlic begins to color, about 2 minutes. Mash the anchovies and add the cauliflower, mashing it into small pea-size pieces. Add ¼ teaspoon hot red pepper flakes and season with salt. Cook for several minutes more. Add 1 cup of the pasta cooking liquid, then the cooked and drained pasta. Toss thoroughly with ¼ cup toasted coarse fresh bread crumbs and garnish with chopped parsley.

VARIATIONS:

- Add ½ cup golden raisins along with the garlic and ½ cup toasted pine nuts with the bread crumbs.
- Add 1 cup diced red bell pepper, ½ cup green or black pitted olives, and 1 coarsely chopped ripe tomato along with the red pepper flakes; omit the pasta water and bread crumbs.

PASTA SAUCE WITH
TUNA, CAPERS, OLIVE, AND TOMATO

Gently cook 2 sliced garlic cloves in 2 tablespoons olive oil until just browned, about 2 minutes. Add 1 drained 7-ounce can of oil-packed Italian tuna, 2 tablespoons of drained capers, 1 cup pitted and chopped green or black olives, and 1 cup chopped fresh tomato. Cook for several minutes over medium heat. Add 1 cup of the pasta cooking water, then the cooked and drained pasta. Heat thoroughly. Garnish with a mixture of chopped herbs such as parsley, thyme, oregano, and basil.

PASTA SAUCE WITH
TAPENADE, ORANGE ZEST, OLIVES, AND CHEESE

Add ½ cup of tapenade to cooked and drained pasta along with 1 cup of the pasta cooking water. Toss to coat. Add the zest of 1 orange and ½ cup pitted and chopped olives, either black or green. Cook for several minutes. Serve garnished with freshly grated Parmesan cheese and chopped basil or parsley.

Pasta Sauce with Walnuts, Garlic, Bread Crumbs, Cheese, and Parsley

This recipe is the gift of my dear friend, Faith Echtermeyer, a blithe and generous-spirited cook who routinely turns out great food with minimal fuss. She calls this "Pasta Nada" or "pasta from nothing." It's truly more than the sum of its parts.

Gently sauté 2 sliced garlic cloves in ¼ cup olive oil until just golden, about 2 minutes. Add 1½ cups coarsely chopped and lightly toasted walnuts and ¼ cup lightly toasted coarse fresh bread crumbs. Add the cooked and drained pasta and toss thoroughly. Garnish with shaved Parmesan cheese and lots of chopped flat-leaf parsley.

Pasta Sauce with Pancetta, Shallots, Golden Raisins, Rosemary, and Balsamic Vinegar

Cut 5 ounces pancetta into small dice and sauté over medium-high heat until soft to render the fat. Discard all but 2 tablespoons of the fat and set aside the pancetta pieces to drain. Add 1 tablespoon unsalted butter and 6 chopped shallots and sauté with 2 tablespoons chopped fresh rosemary over low heat until brown and caramelized, about 35 to 40 minutes. Add the reserved pancetta, ½ cup golden raisins, and 1 teaspoon balsamic vinegar. Toss with cooked and drained pasta and serve at once garnished with crumbled Gorgonzola cheese.

VARIATION: Add sautéed wild and/or cultivated mushrooms or cooked artichoke hearts cut into quarters; substitute Parmesan cheese for the Gorgonzola.

PASTA SAUCE WITH BEAN SPROUTS, GREENS, SHIITAKE MUSHROOMS, AND SESAME SEEDS

A sauce with a satisfying Asian savor.

In 2 tablespoons peanut oil, sauté 6 sliced garlic cloves and 1 tablespoon grated fresh ginger over medium heat until lightly browned, about 1 minute. Add ½ pound sliced shiitake mushroom caps and cook over high heat until the mushroom liquid is released, about 4 to 5 minutes. Add 4 cups greens such as bok choy, Swiss chard, spinach, arugula, or escarole and 1 cup bean sprouts. Cook, covered, just until the greens have wilted, about 3 to 4 minutes. Add 1½ tablespoons tamari and 1 tablespoon sesame oil. Add the cooked and drained pasta and toss. Garnish with ¼ cup toasted sesame seeds.

VARIATIONS:

- Add salted cashews.
- Substitute ½ teaspoon hot red pepper flakes for the ginger and garnish with Parmesan cheese instead of the sesame seeds.

Salads Large and Small

Avocado-Papaya Salad

Thai Carrot Salad

Hot-Sweet Coleslaw with Caramelized Almonds

Endive and Watercress Salad with Oranges and Fennel

Mixed Greens with Tapenade Vinaigrette

Jerusalem Artichoke, Radish, and Watercress Salad

Jicama and Toasted Pumpkin Seed Salad with Orange-Garlic Vinaigrette

Parsley and Mint Salad

Asian Sesame Noodle Salad

Salad of Black-Eyed Peas and Vegetables

Catahoula's Tomatoes-in-All-Their-Glory Salad

Warm Beet Salad with Walnuts and Dill

Chiffonade of Radicchio with Baked Goat Cheese

Thai-Inspired Seafood Salad

Mushroom Salad

Vegetable Juice Dressings and Sauces

  Tomato-Basil Vinaigrette

  Tomato, Red Pepper, and Cumin Vinaigrette

  Ginger-Carrot Vinaigrette

  Cucumber-Dill Sauce

Avocado-Papaya Salad

Serve this colorful salad just as it is or topped with grilled shrimp or scallops or some fresh crabmeat.

1	ripe papaya, halved lengthwise, seeds and strings removed
	Juice of 1 lemon
1	large ripe avocado, halved lengthwise and pitted
1½	tablespoons seasoned rice vinegar
¼	cup extra-virgin olive oil
½	teaspoon Dijon mustard
	Salt and freshly ground black pepper to taste
2	cups torn mixed greens in bite-size pieces
2	tablespoons chopped fresh chives

With a sharp knife, cut ¼-inch-thick slices of the papaya lengthwise through to the skin. Detach the slices from the skin with a large soupspoon. Sprinkle with half the lemon juice. Repeat with the avocado halves.

To make the dressing, combine the vinegar, oil, and mustard in a small bowl. Season with salt and pepper.

Divide the greens between 2 salad plates. Arrange alternating papaya and avocado slices on the greens and pour some of the dressing over each serving. Garnish with the chives and, if you are serving it, the seafood.

GREEN LENTIL AND

ESCAROLE SOUP

•

SEAWEED FOUGASSE

•

AVOCADO-PAPAYA SALAD

•

BLACK-SESAME TUILES

WITH ICE CREAM

WINE SUGGESTIONS:
A DRIER CALIFORNIA
ROSÉ OR BLUSH WINE

The Good Avocado

Everyone knows avocados are high in fat, but a case can be made that avocados are good for you despite the fact that an average-size fruit contains about 275 calories (17 calories a slice) and about 7 to 23 percent fat, depending on type. Avocados have no cholesterol, and like olive oil, their fat is mainly the healthy monosaturated type. They are highly nutritious, rich in eight essential vitamins, especially A (beta-carotene), C, and E, and supply five minerals, particularly potassium.

Avocados are a native American fruit. U.S. markets carry three types: the Mexican, grown largely in California; the West Indian, grown only in Florida; and an intermediate strain, the Guatemalan, raised in both states. Avocados of one variety or another are in season all year long, the Florida crop peaking in October, the Californian running from February through September. The pebbly-skinned dark green Hass makes up 75 percent of the California crop and is the creamiest and richest of all; other California avocados include the excellent Fuerte, the Bacon, the Zutano, and the Rincon. Florida's avocados—lighter green, with a shiny skin—have a higher water content and often a very large pit. The Booth and Lula varieties are the most flavorful.

THAI CARROT SALAD

I first tasted a salad like this in a Thai restaurant in Marin County. It was so spirited and refreshing—so mercifully unlike the standard delicatessen mix of limp carrots and raisins adrift in highly questionable mayonnaise—that I immediately set about devising a version of my own. Use more pepper flakes for a zingier salad, less for a milder one. The temperature setting here is medium-hot.

1	pound carrots, peeled/cut into thin strands on a Benriner cutter (see note on page 97) or grated
¼	cup unseasoned rice vinegar
	Juice of 1 lime, about 2 to 3 tablespoons
1	tablespoon grated lime zest
2	tablespoons honey
¼	teaspoon hot red pepper flakes
1½	cups Spanish peanuts, coarsely chopped
¼	cup crystallized ginger, julienned
¼	cup pepitas (roasted pumpkin seeds)
¼	cup cilantro leaves
2	tablespoons chopped fresh mint

Place the carrots in a large mixing bowl. Blend together the vinegar, lime juice, lime zest, honey, and red pepper flakes. Add the dressing to the carrot mixture and let stand for about 15 minutes. Toss in the remaining ingredients at the last minute.

HOT-SWEET COLESLAW WITH CARAMELIZED ALMONDS

SERVES 6

Thin strips of jícama and fennel give this version of classic coleslaw extra crunch. The spicy mayonnaise and sugared almonds provide the jolts of hot and sweet. This is a truly addictive combination.

Caramelized Almonds

2   tablespoons sugar
2   tablespoons water
¾   cup blanched almonds
1   teaspoon coarse salt or more to taste

Hot-Sweet Mayonnaise

¾   cup low-fat store-bought or homemade mayonnaise
¼   cup sour cream or yogurt
1   teaspoon honey
¾   teaspoon cayenne pepper

Vegetables

1   cup cored and thinly sliced green cabbage
1   cup cored and thinly sliced red cabbage
2   tablespoons finely minced onion or shallot
2   cups peeled and julienned jícama
1   cup grated carrot
1   cup thinly sliced fennel, preferably sliced on a
     mandoline or similar slicer

To caramelize the almonds, combine the sugar and water in a medium skillet and cook over medium-high heat until the mixture begins to bubble and brown slightly, about 3 minutes. Do not stir, but swirl the pan by the handle. Add the almonds and toss to coat. Immediately remove the nuts from the skillet and spread them to cool on a cookie sheet lined with foil. Sprin-

MINTED SNOW PEA AND

POTATO SOUP

•

WILD MUSHROOM

SALLY LUNN

•

HOT-SWEET COLESLAW WITH

CARAMELIZED ALMONDS

•

PERFECT GINGERBREAD

•

DRIED FRUIT WITH

GOOD SPIRITS

WINE SUGGESTIONS:

A CALIFORNIA VIOGNIER OR

PINOT BLANC

kle with coarse salt. (You can do this ahead of time; stored in an airtight container, the nuts will keep for several weeks.)

In a small bowl, blend all the ingredients for the mayonnaise in the order listed.

In a large mixing bowl, combine the prepared vegetables and the mayonnaise. Cover and allow to rest in the refrigerator for at least 30 minutes. Fold in the almonds just before serving.

Endive and Watercress Salad with Oranges and Fennel

SERVES 6

- 2 bunches of watercress
- 3 heads of Belgian endive
- 1 medium fennel bulb
- 2 large navel oranges
- ¼ cup fruity olive oil
  Salt and freshly ground black pepper to taste
- 1 tablespoon minced fresh tarragon

Remove the leaves from the watercress. Cut out the cores of the endive and discard. Chop the endive leaves into ¼-inch pieces. Finely cut the fennel into crosswise slices, discarding the core. Toss the greens and fennel together in a salad bowl.

Over a bowl to catch the juice, peel the oranges with a knife, cutting off the membrane with the skin. Remove the sections by cutting between membranes and popping them out. Reserve the juice. Add the orange sections to the greens and fennel.

Whisk together the olive oil, salt, pepper, tarragon, and 2 tablespoons of the reserved orange juice. Drizzle the dressing over the salad and toss well.

SPRINGWATER MUSHROOM

BROTH

•

CELERY ROOT AND

PARSNIP GRATIN

•

RUTABAGAS WITH GOLDEN

DELICIOUS APPLES

•

ENDIVE AND WATERCRESS

SALAD WITH ORANGES

AND FENNEL

•

PEARS BAKED IN CREAM

WINE SUGGESTIONS:
A FRESH FRENCH VOUVRAY OR
AN OFF-DRY CALIFORNIA
CHENIN BLANC

Mixed Greens with Tapenade Vinaigrette

Lusty tapenade from the south of France comes in green or purple, the green made with green olives, the purple, the classic version, made with black.

2   garlic cloves, peeled
⅔   cup extra-virgin olive oil
3   tablespoons balsamic vinegar
2   tablespoons drained capers
3   tablespoons tapenade made with green or black olives
6 to 8 cups mixed greens
    Salt and freshly ground black pepper to taste

Rub the garlic thoroughly around the inside of a wooden salad bowl; discard. In the bottom of the bowl, combine the oil, vinegar, capers, and tapenade; whisk together until emulsified. Just before serving, add the greens and toss well. Season to taste with salt and pepper.

Jerusalem Artichoke, Radish, and Watercress Salad

SERVES 6

Crisp and crunchy, this is a perfect little fresh-as-a-garden salad to have before or after a heavy meal.

In case you wondered, Jerusalem artichokes, or sunchokes, are neither artichokes nor from Jerusalem. They are the knobby roots of a native American sunflower, surprisingly sweet and crispy, with translucent flesh. Added raw to salads, their appealing texture is akin to that of a water chestnut. They pickle well, are very good roasted whole or sautéed, and make a nice addition to stir-fries. When shopping for these tubers, select large firm knobs with clear, unblemished golden skin.

1   pound Jerusalem artichokes
2   bunches of radishes, about 12 medium, rinsed and
        sliced paper-thin
2   large bunches of watercress, tough stems removed
     Olive oil
     Fresh lemon juice
     Salt and freshly ground black pepper to taste
     Thinly shaved Parmesan cheese

Peel the Jerusalem artichokes if the skins are tough. Cut into paper-thin slices on a mandoline or with a knife.

Toss the Jerusalem artichokes, radishes, and watercress together in a salad bowl.

In a small bowl, whisk together the oil, lemon juice, and salt and pepper. Dress the salad and add the Parmesan shavings just before serving.

CANTALOUPE WITH
BLACK OLIVES

•

RISOTTO WITH LEMON
AND HERBS

•

JERUSALEM ARTICHOKE,
RADISH, AND
WATERCRESS SALAD

•

CHOCOLATE PUDDING CAKE

WINE SUGGESTIONS:
A CALIFORNIA RIESLING OR A
GERMAN KABINETT
MIT PRÄDIKAT

Jícama and Toasted Pumpkin Seed Salad with Orange-Garlic Vinaigrette

Wine suggestions:
Beer, preferably an amber
beer served with wedges of
lime, would be best with this
menu. Or try a young
Zinfandel or
Australian Shiraz.

This flavorful salad of southwestern elements is built around the refreshing jícama, the crisp, slightly sweet tuber that looks like a drab potato but has a texture more like a tender radish. Peel the thin skin, then squeeze some lime juice and a little chili powder over its snowy whiteness for a quick low-calorie snack or add it to salads for crunch. Long a staple in California markets, jícama is now available countrywide. Choose the smallest jícama you can find since the giant ones tend to be woody. Don't wash the jícama before storing, or it will get soggy. You can make the dressing several hours ahead.

Orange-Garlic Vinaigrette

½   cup packed fresh mint leaves
1   teaspoon finely grated orange zest
1   tablespoon frozen orange juice concentrate
2   teaspoons rice or white vinegar
1   garlic clove, minced
½   cup vegetable oil

Salad

2   cups peeled and julienned jícama
4   cups torn romaine lettuce in bite-size pieces
¼   cup pumpkin seeds, toasted

Place the vinaigrette ingredients in a blender and blend until emulsified.

Combine the vegetables and pumpkin seeds in a salad bowl and toss with the dressing immediately before serving.

Mixing Salad Greens

You might wonder which salad greens to include when I call for "mixed greens" in a recipe. The field is wide open, of course, but in my opinion a well-considered selection from the following list will have visual interest, balance, and a pleasing variety of leaf forms, colors, flavors, and textures. Mix for contrast if a fine balance is your goal or select three or more greens for what they might have in common; for instance, a trio of bitter greens such as radicchio, endive, and arugula is assertive and just right after a rich main course.

Do not drown delicately flavored tender greens in a heavy dressing. Save your more robust dressings for greens with substantial texture or piquancy. For lightness combined with intense flavor, try one of the vegetable juice dressings later in this chapter.

Mizuna: feathery in appearance with a tangy, delicate mustard flavor and mild taste
Lolla rossa lettuce: frilled leaves, light and crunchy; eye-catching
Pea shoots: tender leaves and growing tips of young pea vines; delicate pea flavor
Belgian endive: slightly bitter, succulent, and crunchy
Arugula (rocket, roquette, rugula, rucola): peppery, ranging from mild to sharp
Oak leaf lettuce: buttery, tender, and sweet; red or green
Frisée (curly endive): finely cut leaves; slightly bitter, mildly nutty
Mâche (corn salad, lamb's lettuce): very delicate, buttery, tender

Not finding these, by all means use a mixture of any other young greens, the freshest you can buy.

Parsley and Mint Salad

If you use parsley strictly as an herb or a garnish, you'll be surprised at how well it works as the main ingredient in a salad. This traditional Italian dish is delicious made with either curly- or flat-leaf parsley, though for texture and taste I'm partial to a mix of the two. It's great served alongside fried foods or with the rich *Farci* with Fresh White Cheese.

Parsley is one of the most nutritious greens around, loaded with chlorophyll, vitamin C, and particularly vitamin A, of which it is the world's single richest plant source. Mint is its natural companion in the garden as well as the salad bowl.

1 bunch of curly-leaf parsley, stemmed
1 bunch of flat-leaf parsley, stemmed
1 packed cup fresh mint leaves
Thinly shaved Parmesan cheese for garnish

Lemon-Anchovy Dressing

Juice of 1 lemon
1 large garlic clove, minced
3 anchovy fillets, drained and mashed
1 tablespoon capers, preferably salt-packed and rinsed,* minced if large
½ cup extra-virgin olive oil

Toss the parsley with the mint leaves in a salad bowl.

To make the dressing, mash the lemon juice with the garlic and anchovies in a small bowl to make a smooth paste. Add the capers. Add the oil in a steady stream, beating all the time until the oil is emulsified. Pour the dressing over the parsley and mint and toss to coat evenly.

Shave in some Parmesan just before serving or pass a small bowl of shavings and let people add as much as they wish.

*The piquant flavor of the little buds of the caper bush is overwhelmed when packed in brine, so a much better choice are the salt-packed capers sold in bulk in a range of sizes at a growing number of specialty stores and Italian markets. Give these a good rinsing to remove the salt, and you will be rewarded with authentic caper flavor and a nice, firm texture. Salt-packed capers can be mail-ordered for $12 a pound from Dean & Deluca in New York (800-221-7714) and from Cantinetta Tra Vigne in St. Helena, California (707-963-8888).

Asian Sesame Noodle Salad

SERVES 4 TO 6

Everyone loves this. Pair it with other Asia-influenced dishes such as the Cilantro Mousse and the Thai-Inspired Seafood Salad.

1   cup peanut oil
3   tablespoons unseasoned rice vinegar
3   tablespoons soy sauce
1   teaspoon Asian sesame oil
1   tablespoon lightly toasted sesame seeds, preferably black
1   tablespoon minced garlic
1   tablespoon peeled and grated fresh ginger
1   tablespoon finely chopped scallion, both white and green parts
1   tablespoon minced cilantro leaves
1   pound capellini or other thin pasta, cooked until al dente and drained

In a medium bowl, combine all the ingredients except the pasta in the order listed. Pour the sauce over the cooked pasta and toss to coat. Serve warm or at room temperature.

CILANTRO MOUSSE

•

ASIAN SESAME

NOODLE SALAD

•

THAI-INSPIRED

SEAFOOD SALAD

•

MANGO SALSA

•

CARDAMOM SHORTBREAD

COOKIES WITH

COCONUT ICE CREAM

WINE SUGGESTIONS:
A LIGHTER-BODIED BEER
OR AN OFF-DRY WHITE WINE
SUCH AS A CALIFORNIA
GEWÜRZTRAMINER WITH A
TOUCH OF SWEETNESS

SALAD OF BLACK-EYED PEAS AND VEGETABLES

SERVES 6

Bacon and bitter greens are the traditional southern companions for black-eyed peas. In this recipe I have used pancetta and peppery watercress or arugula instead. This makes an excellent luncheon dish or light summer dinner.

1   cup dried black-eyed peas
6   thin slices pancetta, ¼ pound
1   large red bell pepper, in pea-size dice
2   small zucchini, about ½ pound, in pea-size dice
1   medium carrot, in pea-size dice
2   celery stalks, in pea-size dice
1   bunch of watercress or arugula, about 2 cups
    Salt and freshly ground black pepper to taste
1   small head of curly endive, about 2 cups

Walnut Vinaigrette

2   tablespoons red balsamic vinegar
1   tablespoon grainy Dijon-style mustard
⅓   cup walnut oil
3   tablespoons minced shallots
2   tablespoons walnuts, chopped

In a large saucepan, simmer the peas in water to cover by 2 inches for about 30 minutes or until just tender. Meanwhile, sauté the pancetta in a nonstick pan over medium-high heat until crisp, about 6 minutes. Tilt the pan and, using a crumpled-up paper towel, soak up all the fat; discard.

Add the red pepper, zucchini, carrot, and celery to the pancetta and cook for 2 to 3 minutes.

Make the Walnut Vinaigrette in a small bowl, whisking together the vinegar and mustard. Slowly add the oil until emulsified. Stir in the shallots and nuts and set aside.

Drain the peas and, while they are still warm, combine them with the

TOMATO ASPIC WITH SAFFRON-

HERB MAYONNAISE

•

SALAD OF BLACK-EYED PEAS

AND VEGETABLES

•

ANGEL BISCUITS

•

PEACH AND

BLUEBERRY BUCKLE

WINE SUGGESTIONS:
CHIANTI CLASSICO OR A
CENTRAL OR SOUTHERN
SPANISH RIOJA

pancetta and vegetables in a large serving bowl. Dress with half the vinaigrette; mix gently.

When the pea mixture has cooled slightly, add half the watercress. Season with salt and pepper. Arrange the curly endive and remaining watercress on a large serving platter. Spoon the salad on top and dress with the remaining vinaigrette.

CATAHOULA'S TOMATOES-IN-ALL-THEIR-GLORY SALAD

SERVES 4

". . . Tomato slices, red and thick and ripe, and heavy as a chop."—Thomas Wolfe

Daily salads of summer's dead-ripe garden tomatoes are, for me, one of the enduring pleasures of the season. A combination of juicy yellow- and red-fleshed tomatoes makes an irresistible sunburst of warm color on a platter, but for the deepest flavor of all I often opt for the reds alone. Lemon Boy is great, but Better Boy is, well, better. Most of the old-fashioned beefsteak varieties have the high acid and tangy tart-sweet taste I like most in a tomato. Well-named Early Girl and brightly striped Tigerella are other winners.

This is not so much a salad as an unbeatable, tried-and-true way to bring out the best in high summer's great tomatoes—vine-ripened, sliced, and lightly dressed. In addition to the classic basil, oil, and vinegar, try adding some fresh corn cut from the cob, a scoop of fresh ricotta cheese, and a sprinkling of reduced balsamic vinegar. The Cornmeal Waffles (on page 207) add just the right crunch.

2	**ripe red tomatoes, about 1 pound**
2	**ripe yellow tomatoes, about 1 pound**
	Salt and freshly ground black pepper to taste
½	**cup balsamic vinegar, reduced over high heat to ¼ cup**
	Extra-virgin olive oil
	Mixed baby lettuces
	Finely chopped fresh basil leaves

Thinly slice the tomatoes and overlap them on a serving platter. Season with salt and pepper. Drizzle a small amount of the vinegar syrup over them if you wish and an equal amount of olive oil. Garnishes: fresh corn kernels, ricotta cheese, mixed baby lettuces, and finely chopped fresh basil leaves.

Variation: Tuck thick slices of peeled red onion between the slices of tomato.

FAVA BEANS À LA GRECQUE

•

RISOTTO WITH SWEET CORN

•

CATAHOULA'S TOMATOES-IN-ALL-THEIR-GLORY SALAD

•

STRAWBERRIES IN LEMON VERBENA WITH FRESH CHEESE ICE CREAM

WINE SUGGESTIONS:
A CALIFORNIA CHARDONNAY OR A FRENCH MEURSAULT OR A WELL-MADE POUILLY-FUISSÉ

Warm Beet Salad with Walnuts and Dill

SERVES 6

A wonderful wintertime salad.

Baking or roasting beets produces the best flavor but requires a long cooking time. The answer throughout France is the freshly roasted beets found in the markets, ready to take home for use in salads or soups. Here in America microwaving is a fast and easy compromise with little sacrifice in taste.

Beets grow in dense clusters; baby beets arrive in markets whenever the crop is thinned. Look for bunches of uniformly sized beets so they will cook evenly.

3½   **pounds baby beets, about 6 cups, greens reserved**
¼   **cup seasoned rice vinegar**
1   **tablespoon red wine vinegar**
2 to 3 **tablespoons walnut oil**
¼   **cup chicken stock, preferably homemade**
½   **teaspoon salt**
    Freshly ground black pepper to taste
¼   **cup lightly toasted chopped walnuts**
2   **tablespoons chopped fresh dill**

Wash the beet greens and trim them down to 1 inch. Cut the greens into ribbons, discarding the stems or setting them aside for another use. Scrub the beets well and arrange in a circle on a microwave-safe dish. Cover with plastic wrap and cook at 100 percent power for 9 minutes, rotating the dish every 3 minutes or placing on a carousel. Watch carefully so smaller beets don't get overdone; larger beets may take a little longer. Or bake the beets, wrapped in aluminum foil, in a preheated 375°F oven until tender, about 1 hour. Set aside until cool enough to peel. Discard the skins and quarter all but 2 beets.

To make the dressing, puree the 2 whole beets in a blender or food processor with the vinegars and oil.

In a large skillet, simmer the beet greens in the chicken stock for 5 minutes or until just wilted. Add the quartered beets and fold in about two thirds of the dressing. Season with salt and pepper. Toss until the beets are heated through.

Arrange some of the greens on each salad plate. Arrange 4 or 5 beet quarters in a spiral pattern around the outer edge of the greens. Decorate with a few chopped walnuts and some dill. Drizzle a teaspoon of the remaining beet dressing on top. (The dressing is quite thick; if you like a thinner dressing, use more oil.)

Beet Basics

Don't avoid beets just because their extravagant color bleeds onto kitchen towels, hands, and fingernails. To avoid stains, wear rubber gloves or, first, trim beet stems to within an inch of the crowns and then, when the beets have cooked, hold them in paper towels, grasp the skin between thumb and forefinger, and peel it away.

Remember to slice beets on a ceramic plate rather than a wood chopping block. Use lemon juice to help remove any stains on your hands.

Boiling beets leeches out some of the flavor. Steaming minimizes bleeding and concentrates flavor but takes 30 to 45 minutes; quarter or halve very large beets and steam them until done. Roasting beets in their skins in the oven produces the most intense flavor of all, concentrating the natural sugars and yielding a rich, sweet taste; skins come out crisp, interiors soft and moist. At 375°F, small beets require about 1 hour, larger ones 15 to 20 minutes more. For microwave directions, see Warm Beet Salad with Walnuts and Dill.

Buy beets with fresh-looking leaves. This way you get two vegetables in one. Baby beets and medium-sized beets have equally good flavor, but large beets can be tough and woody. Three heirloom strains are making their first inroads into American markets: golden beets, with flesh that is close to orange, have a sweet, delicate taste; *Barbietola di Chioggia,* or "candy-cane," is a handsome beet with concentric rings of purple and white that turn pale pink when cooked; *Albina Vereduna* has sweet ice-white flesh, and it won't stain your hands.

Grate raw beets into salads for delicious crunch and earthy aftertaste.

CHIFFONADE OF RADICCHIO WITH BAKED GOAT CHEESE

SERVES 6

Radicchio, the status salad stuff of the eighties, is happily more available than in those years, less pricey, and just as welcome for its clean bite and elegant claret color. The variety seen most often in markets is the pretty purple-and-ivory streaked radicchio di Chioggia. Look for perky, unblemished specimens with a firm white base. If only rusty-looking heads are available, you can remove the tired outer leaves and usually find more than acceptable inner leaves.

If you enjoy the rich taste of pancetta, a small amount will marry well with the assertive flavors of the radicchio and cheese.

2	tablespoons vegetable oil or 2 ounces pancetta or lean bacon, optional, cut into small pieces
2	heads of radicchio, ½ pound each, trimmed and cut into ½-inch-wide strips
12	Greek olives, pitted and coarsely chopped
2	teaspoons drained capers
1	tablespoon balsamic vinegar
2	teaspoons cider vinegar
½	teaspoon salt
	Freshly ground black pepper to taste
	Minced parsley

Baked Goat Cheese

6	rounds of fresh goat cheese, each 2½ inches in diameter, ½ inch thick, and about 1 ounce
1½	cups fresh bread crumbs

In a large cast-iron skillet, heat the vegetable oil over medium heat. (If you're using the pancetta, brown the pieces in the skillet over medium-high heat. Set the browned pieces to the side and pour off all but 2 table-

CARROT-RHUBARB SOUP WITH

CINNAMON CROUTONS

•

ROASTED BARLEY AND

WILD MUSHROOM PILAF

•

CHIFFONADE OF RADICCHIO

WITH BAKED GOAT CHEESE

•

MAPLE PEARS WITH

CARDAMOM CREAM

WINE SUGGESTIONS:
A SPANISH RIOJA OR A
MEDIUM-BODIED
CALIFORNIA NEBBIOLO

spoons of the rendered fat.) Add the radicchio and cook until browned, about 5 minutes.

In a large serving bowl, whisk together the olives, capers, vinegars, salt, and pepper. Add the radicchio and the pancetta if you're using it; toss gently. Sprinkle with parsley.

Preheat the oven to 400°F.

Carefully dip the goat cheese rounds in the bread crumbs, coating all sides. Arrange on a lightly oiled baking sheet and bake in the middle of the oven for about 5 to 6 minutes, until the cheese is golden brown. Serve at once with the radicchio and some lightly toasted croutons or bread.

Pancetta and Its Substitutes

Magnificent for adding substance and subtle flavor to mostly meatless dishes, pancetta is unsmoked Italian bacon that is cured with salt and spices (usually cloves and peppercorns) and then rolled into a log shape.

Pancetta is stocked mainly in specialty stores, Italian delicatessens, or supermarkets in areas with large Italian-American populations, so the question of a substitute arises. Pancetta has no American equivalent, though, like American bacon, it is cut from the belly of the pig. Salt pork by itself is far too fatty and salty, but mix it with an equal quantity of lean boiled ham, and you have an acceptable substitute. Perhaps the best alternative is good-quality lean American breakfast bacon; it shares pancetta's texture and fat content. But it's much saltier, so drop it in boiling water for about a minute and drain before using.

If you can't find pancetta locally, you can mail-order it in bulk from Balducci's (800-225-3822), a leading New York gourmet store. When the pancetta arrives, freeze it in small quantities and defrost as needed.

Thai-Inspired Seafood Salad

SERVES 6

For a delightful summer luncheon or light dinner of East-West flavorings, serve this salad with the Cilantro Mousse and the Asian Sesame Noodle Salad. At first glance this may appear complicated, but it can be prepared in a series of quick and easy steps.

Dressing

½ cup plus 1 tablespoon fresh lime juice, from about 3 limes
2 tablespoons Thai fish sauce*
2 tablespoons dark brown sugar
2 scallions, finely chopped
1 teaspoon molasses

Fried Wonton Wrappers

1 cup peanut oil
30 3-inch-square wonton wrappers, the thinnest you can find, cut into ½-inch strips

Salad

1 small Napa cabbage, outer leaves removed, cored, and cut into ½-inch strips
2 firm ripe tomatoes, cut into ½-inch dice
1 firm ripe papaya, peeled, seeded, and chopped into ½-inch pieces
½ pound large shrimp, peeled with tails left on
½ pound bay scallops
1 head of butter lettuce, leaves separated
   Lime slices and tomato slices for garnish

Combine all the dressing ingredients in a small bowl in the order listed. Whisk together and set aside. You can make the dressing an hour ahead.

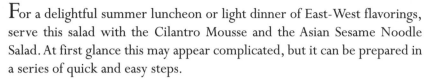

Wine suggestions:
A lighter-bodied beer or an off-dry white wine such as a California Gewürztraminer with a touch of sweetness

Heat the oil until hot but not smoking in a wok or large skillet. You can test the temperature of the oil by frying one wonton. It is hot enough if the wonton begins to sizzle as soon as it hits the oil. Fry the wonton strips a few at a time, moving them around with tongs or a wooden spoon, until they begin to brown, about 1 minute. Drain on paper towels. Repeat with the remaining strips, making sure that the oil is hot before adding each new batch. Set aside.

To prepare the salad, prepare a grill.

In a large bowl, combine the cabbage, tomatoes, and papaya. Toss with the dressing, cover, and chill.

Grill the shrimp and scallops 4 inches from a medium-high flame, turning once, for about 4 minutes or until just cooked.

Arrange a few lettuce leaves on individual serving plates. Toss the dressed cabbage mixture again and divide it among the plates. Distribute several shrimp and scallops over each serving and decorate with Fried Wonton Wrappers, lime slices, and tomato slices.

*Thai cooking's trademark "cool heat" derives much of its character from the blending of salty, sour, sweet, and hot seasonings. Fish sauce, called *nam pla* in Thailand, *nuoc nam* in Vietnam, provides the salty component in innumerable Southeast Asian dishes; in Thailand bottles of it grace every tabletop just as ketchup is set out on tables here or soy sauce in China. To produce the condiment, layers of fish and salt are placed in large jars or barrels and fermented for at least 3 months before the accumulated brown liquid is drained off and bottled. The aroma is pungent, the flavor subtly briny. Fish sauce is inexpensive, and you can buy it at Asian groceries or well-stocked gourmet shops. Anzen Groceries and Imports (736 N.E. Martin Luther King Jr. Blvd., Portland, OR 97232; 503-233-5111) carries it if you can't find it locally. An open bottle will keep almost indefinitely in the refrigerator.

Mushroom Salad

The subtle earthy flavors of the mushrooms sing out against the simple background of the sage. The walnut oil dressing works as a flavor bridge. Robust and satisfying.

¼   **cup extra-virgin olive oil**
2   **tablespoons unsalted butter**
2 to 3 **pounds assorted mushrooms, such as porcini, shiitake, cremini, and white, thinly sliced**
¼   **cup minced shallots**
1   **garlic clove, minced**
3   **tablespoons dry sherry, such as Amontillado**
    Salt and freshly ground black pepper to taste
6   **cups red leaf lettuce, about ½ pound**
5   **tablespoons walnut oil**
2   **teaspoons balsamic vinegar**
1   **cup lightly toasted walnuts, coarsely chopped**
4 to 5 **fresh sage leaves, cut into ribbons**
¼   **pound Parmesan cheese, shaved**

In a large sauté pan, heat the oil and butter together. Add the mushrooms, shallots, and garlic and sauté over medium-high heat for about 6 minutes to release the juices. Continue cooking, stirring frequently, until all liquid is absorbed and the mushrooms begin to brown, about 8 minutes longer. Add the sherry and cook until it has evaporated, about 3 minutes. Season with salt and pepper.

Arrange a few of the lettuce leaves on individual salad plates. Divide the mushrooms evenly among the plates. Whisk together the oil and vinegar and pour over the mushrooms and lettuce. Decorate with walnuts, sage, and a few Parmesan shavings.

Vegetable Juice Dressings and Sauces

"I'll just have a salad" used to be the best riposte of health-conscious eaters when confronted with menus top-heavy with high-fat, high-calorie treats. Now, sad to say, we know that even a few tablespoons of an ordinary vinaigrette (three parts oil to one part vinegar) can contain a whole day's recommended fat allowance.

For a healthier salad that sacrifices nothing in flavor, look to the possibilities of vegetable juice–based vinaigrettes and sauces, surely one of the stellar components of today's new-and-improved vegetable cookery. By reducing or eliminating the oil in standard vinaigrettes and substituting the fresh juice of vegetables, you can enjoy lovely light dressings that supply both body and a luminous depth of flavor that literally trick the palate into thinking oil is present. These dressings do double duty as the base for steaming shellfish or, reduced to a thicker consistency, as sauces for fish or chicken. Flavored with a drop or two of an herb- or spice-infused oil, such sauces can be pooled under foods or drizzled directly onto them.

For best results with these dressings and sauces, you will need a good juicer or, better yet, a juice extractor. These sturdy machines are responsible for a good deal of the hidden magic in the mostly-vegetarian kitchen and are well worth the initial investment. (For other uses for juicers and buying recommendations, see page 132.)

Vegetable-based vinaigrettes and sauces are best made within three or four hours before using.

Here are a few of my favorite juice-based dressings along with a cooling sauce for summer vegetables and grilled seafood. Feel free to experiment and come up with combinations of your own.

Tomato-Basil Vinaigrette

This winning combination is delicious on salad greens, pasta, and seafood. Unbeatable as the dressing for a Tuscan-style bread salad.

- 2 large ripe tomatoes, juiced, about 1 cup
- 1 teaspoon grated orange zest
- 2 tablespoons fresh orange juice
- 1 tablespoon chopped fresh basil
- ½ tablespoon chopped fresh mint
- 1 scallion, minced
- 1 teaspoon olive oil or vegetable oil, optional
  Salt and freshly ground black pepper to taste

In a medium bowl, combine everything but the oil, salt, and pepper. Whisk in the oil, salt, and pepper.

Variation: Substitute tarragon for the basil and mint.

Tomato, Red Pepper, and Cumin Vinaigrette

Makes about 1 cup

Try this on grilled vegetables, a corn salad, beans, or fish.

- 1 large ripe tomato, juiced, about ½ cup
- 2 small or 1 large red bell pepper, juiced, about ½ cup, skimmed of all foam
- 1 teaspoon balsamic vinegar
- ¼ teaspoon ground cumin
- 1 teaspoon walnut or olive oil, optional
  Salt and freshly ground black pepper to taste

In a medium bowl, combine everything but the oil, salt, and pepper. Whisk in the oil, salt, and pepper.

GINGER-CARROT VINAIGRETTE

MAKES 1 CUP

Very good on grilled seafood or chicken or as a base for steaming shellfish.

- 6 medium carrots, juiced, 1 cup, skimmed of all foam
- 1 2-inch piece of fresh ginger, juiced, 1 teaspoon
- ½ teaspoon soy sauce
- ½ teaspoon Asian sesame oil
- ½ teaspoon peanut oil
- 1 tablespoon chopped cilantro

In a medium bowl, combine the juices and soy sauce. Whisk in the oils and cilantro.

CUCUMBER-DILL SAUCE

MAKES 1½ CUPS

This sauce adds sparkle to tomato salads, potatoes, orzo, or grilled seafood.

- 1 large European cucumber, unpeeled and juiced, 1 cup, skimmed of all foam
- 2 tablespoons low-fat plain yogurt
- 2 tablespoons chopped fresh dill
- 1 scallion, minced, both white and green parts
- 1 garlic clove, minced
  Salt and freshly ground black pepper to taste

In a medium bowl, whisk together the cucumber juice and yogurt. Whisk in the remaining ingredients in the order listed.

Breads, Muffins, and Crackers

Chive Popovers

Fennel and Asiago Twists

Seaweed Fougasse

Model Bakery Corn-Chili Muffins

Angel Biscuits

Wild Mushroom Sally Lunn

Parmesan Cake

Savory Wine Biscuits

Sun-Dried Tomato and Gruyère Cheese Puffs

Southern Persimmon Bread with Corn and Black Walnuts

Catahoula's Cornmeal Waffles

CHIVE POPOVERS

This simple batter can be made several days ahead and refrigerated, but for popovers that pop reliably and well, bring made-ahead batter to room temperature and stir well before pouring it into the prepared pan. Add the chives to the batter just before baking.

	Vegetable oil spray
2	**cups all-purpose flour**
1	**teaspoon salt**
6	**extra-large eggs**
2	**cups milk**
6	**tablespoons unsalted butter, melted**
¼	**cup minced chives**

Preheat the oven to 375°F. Coat the wells of a 12-cup muffin pan with vegetable oil spray.

In a mixing bowl, combine the flour and salt. Beat the eggs just to blend and add to the flour along with the milk, melted butter, and chives. Beat just to mix.

Fill each cup half full of batter and bake for 50 to 60 minutes. Cut a slit in the top of each popover during the last 15 minutes of baking to allow steam to escape. Remove from the cups and serve at once.

WARM BEET SALAD WITH

WALNUTS AND DILL

•

Sformato OF CAULIFLOWER

WITH TOMATO-WATERCRESS

CONCASSÉE

•

Sformato OF CARROTS

•

CHIVE POPOVERS

•

FRESH FRUIT WITH

GOOD SPIRITS

WINE SUGGESTIONS:

ROSSO DI MONTALCINO OR A

CALIFORNIA SANGIOVESE

OR A LIGHT- TO MEDIUM-

BODIED ZINFANDEL

Fennel and Asiago Twists

These quick and easy breadsticklike twists are the perfect accompaniment for soups and salads of all types. Best when served right from the oven, they can be made weeks in advance and frozen.

> 1½-pound sheet of prepared puff pastry, homemade or
>   store-bought, thawed for 20 minutes if frozen
> 1   large egg, beaten with 2 drops of water or fresh lemon
>   juice
> ½   cup grated Asiago or Parmesan cheese
> 1½ tablespoons fennel seeds, slightly crushed

Preheat the oven to 400°F.

On a lightly floured surface, roll the pastry sheet into an 18- by 9-inch rectangle; cut the rectangle into 1-inch strips. Twist each strip 6 or 8 turns. Place the twists on an ungreased baking sheet and bake for 12 minutes or until they are puffed and golden. Remove from the oven and lightly brush all over with the egg mixture. Sprinkle with the cheese and fennel seeds. Return to the oven for 2 minutes, watching carefully to make sure they don't burn. Serve at once.

LENTIL PUREE WITH OLIVES

AND ANCHOVIES

•

MINESTRONE WITH ROSEMARY-

CHILI PESTO

•

FENNEL AND ASIAGO TWISTS

•

PINEAPPLE CRUMBLE

WINE SUGGESTIONS:

A MEDIUM-BODIED ZINFANDEL

OR A CHÂTEAUNEUF-DU-PAPE

Seaweed Fougasse

I first ate delicious flat disks of bread flavored with nutrient-rich seaweed in, of all places, Provence. This recipe uses shredded nori, a type of seaweed used primarily to wrap sushi. You can find it in natural foods stores, where it is sold dried and pressed into paper-thin sheets ranging in color from dark purple to black.

Fougasse turns stale quite quickly and is best eaten on the day it is made. However, it does freeze well. To reheat: thaw, then warm, well wrapped in foil, in a 350°F oven.

1½ teaspoons active dry yeast
1¼ cups warm water
2   tablespoons Asian sesame oil
3½ cups unbleached flour, more or less
½   tablespoon sea salt or kosher salt
1   cup shredded nori
1   cup thinly sliced yellow onion
2   tablespoons vegetable oil
     Black sesame seeds

In a small bowl, stir the yeast into ¼ cup of the warm water; let stand for about 10 minutes to proof or until a creamy head forms on top.

Put the remaining cup of water and 1 tablespoon of the sesame oil in a large mixing bowl or in a heavy-duty mixer fitted with a dough hook. Add about a quarter of the flour, the salt, and the nori. Stir until smooth. Beat in the remaining flour a little at a time until it's all used and the dough is lumpy but holds together.

On a lightly floured surface, knead the dough by hand for 8 to 10 minutes, until elastic and smooth, or in a mixer for 6 minutes.

Place the remaining sesame oil in a clean bowl. Place the dough in the bowl and turn several times to coat. Cover tightly and let rise in a warm draft-free place until doubled in bulk, about 1½ hours.

Sauté the onion in the vegetable oil in a small skillet over medium heat for 6 to 8 minutes or until wilted but not browned. Drain and set aside.

Punch the dough down and push and shape it to fit a 10½- by 15½-inch shallow pan. Cover with a clean kitchen towel and let rise for about 30 minutes. Using your fingers, dimple the dough all over. Cover again with the towel and let rise for 30 minutes more.

Preheat the oven to 400°F. Just before baking, brush the dough all over with any remaining oil from the rising bowl. Bake for 18 minutes, then scatter the sautéed onions and sesame seeds on top. Bake for about 2 minutes more, taking care not to let the onions burn. Cool on a wire rack. Serve warm or at room temperature.

The Pizza-Focaccia Puzzle:
Which Is Which?

Fougasse is the French cousin of focaccia, the flat Italian bread so popular in the United States in recent years that it has given pizza a run for its money. What exactly is the difference between the two? Carol Field, author of the classic *The Italian Baker* (Harper & Row, 1985), suggests that in current parlance a dough topped with tomato sauce or cheese is pizza whereas dough with added ingredients kneaded into it is focaccia, or fougasse. Focaccia probably came first, a simple bread puddled with olive oil, sprinkled with fresh herbs, and casually set to bake over embers or in the oven. Thickness and temperature are other ways to distinguish between pizza and its more ancient twin. Pizza crust is traditionally less than ½ inch thick and focaccia about ¾ inch. Pizza has to be hot, but chewy focaccia is satisfying either warm or at room temperature. These distinctions, however, are becoming increasingly blurred as the two bread forms cross-pollinate. A diner at a famous New York pizzeria, when asked the difference between the two, responded simply, "About a buck."

MODEL BAKERY CORN-CHILI MUFFINS

MAKES 24 MUFFINS

Karen Mitchell's Model Bakery in St. Helena, California, would be exemplary anywhere on earth, but fortune has placed it just down the road from where I live. I don't know what I would do without my daily hit of something honest and delectable from its ovens, like these memorable muffins.

3　cups yellow cornmeal
1　cup all-purpose flour
2　tablespoons baking powder
2　teaspoons salt
1　teaspoon freshly ground black pepper
4　large eggs, beaten
2　cups sour cream or low-fat sour cream
¼　pound (1 stick) unsalted butter, melted
½　pound cheddar or Jack cheese, grated
½　cup chopped canned green chilies
6　ounces fresh or frozen corn kernels, ¾ cup

Preheat the oven to 375°F. Line the wells in two 12-cup muffin tins with paper liners.

In a large mixing bowl, combine the cornmeal, flour, baking powder, salt, and pepper. In a separate bowl, mix together the eggs, sour cream, and butter. Fold the wet ingredients into the dry ingredients until just mixed. Fold in the cheese, chilies, and corn. Spoon the batter into the muffin tins, filling them about two-thirds full, and bake for about 18 minutes or until a toothpick inserted into the center of a muffin comes out clean. Cool on a wire rack. Serve warm or at room temperature. They are best eaten the day they are made or may be frozen.

TIERRA FARMS

BLACK BEAN CHILI

•

MODEL BAKERY

CORN-CHILI MUFFINS

•

JÍCAMA AND TOASTED PUMPKIN

SEED SALAD WITH ORANGE-

GARLIC VINAIGRETTE

•

BANANA-COLADA TART

WINE SUGGESTIONS:
BEER, PREFERABLY AN AMBER
BEER SERVED WITH WEDGES OF
LIME, WOULD BE BEST WITH THIS
MENU. OR TRY A YOUNG
ZINFANDEL OR
AUSTRALIAN SHIRAZ.

Angel Biscuits

The recipe for these leavened biscuits was given to me by my mother, Joyce Costner, who received it from my father's mother, our beloved Grandmother Costner. The high-rising biscuits that always appear at Christmas filled with Smithfield ham therefore qualify as a genuine "secret" family recipe. My mother remembers a time when the biscuits rose even higher, but unfortunately my grandmother never revealed that part of the secret.

1	¼-ounce envelope active dry yeast
2	tablespoons warm water
5	cups all-purpose flour
1	teaspoon baking soda
1	tablespoon baking powder
¼	cup sugar
1	teaspoon salt
1	cup solid vegetable shortening
2	cups buttermilk
	Oil for the baking sheet

Preheat the oven to 350°F.

In a small bowl, dissolve the yeast in the water for 10 minutes or until foamy.

Sift the dry ingredients together in a separate bowl. Cut in the shortening until the mixture resembles oatmeal.

Combine the buttermilk and dissolved yeast and add to the dry ingredients. Mix until just blended and gather the dough into a ball. Turn out the dough onto a floured board and knead for 2 minutes. Roll to a thickness of ½ inch. Using a lightly floured 3-inch-round cutter, cut out the biscuits and place close together on a lightly oiled baking sheet. (The biscuits do not need to rise before baking.)

Bake for 12 to 15 minutes or until light golden on top. Remove the biscuits from the oven, split in half, and butter lightly. These are best eaten the day they're made.

Wild Mushroom Sally Lunn

Sally Lunn is the wonderful name of a wonderful southern loaf bread. Although the source of the name has been lost over the years, the rich bread itself is still made according to time-honored recipes handed down from the colonial period in the part of Virginia where I grew up. No doubt Virginia cooks worth their salt will accuse me of "tarting up" a perfected heirloom. To them my apologies, but, served warm or lightly toasted with salad and cheese, this mushroom-laced Sally Lunn is really something special.

This recipe makes a generous loaf. Past its prime, the bread makes excellent croutons.

½   **pound (2 sticks) unsalted butter**
1½ **cups warm milk**
4   **large eggs, lightly beaten**
1   **¼-ounce envelope active dry yeast dissolved in ¼ cup**
      warm water
5 to 6 cups all-purpose flour
2   **teaspoons salt**
1   **pound assorted fresh, wild, or cultivated mushrooms,**
      sliced
      Freshly ground black pepper to taste
      Butter or oil for the pan
1   **large egg beaten with ½ cup milk**

Melt 7 ounces (14 tablespoons) of the butter and combine with the warm milk in a small bowl. Mix well and stir in the eggs and dissolved yeast. Beat in the flour and salt to make a thick batter. Cover the bowl with a kitchen towel and set the dough aside in a warm place to rise until doubled in bulk.

Meanwhile, sauté the mushrooms in the remaining 2 tablespoons butter in a skillet over medium heat until wilted, about 4 minutes. Season with pepper; I like lots.

Punch down the dough and knead in the mushrooms until distributed evenly.

Preheat the oven to 375°F and grease a ring mold or angel food cake

TAPENADE

•

BORSCHT WITH

CABBAGE AND APPLES

•

WILD MUSHROOM

SALLY LUNN

•

JERUSALEM ARTICHOKE,

RADISH, AND

WATERCRESS SALAD

•

PINEAPPLE CRUMBLE

WINE SUGGESTIONS:
A DRY GERMAN RIESLING
(TROCKEN) OR A ROUNDER
ALSATIAN RIESLING

pan. Place the dough in the mold or pan, cover with kitchen towels and let rise again until doubled in bulk. Brush the top with the egg wash. Bake until a toothpick inserted in the center comes out clean, about 1 to 1½ hours. Remove from the pan to a cooling rack. Serve warm or lightly toasted.

Parmesan Cake

This delicate cakelike bread is perfect sliced, toasted, smeared with cheese or left plain, and served with a salad course.

¼	pound (1 stick) unsalted butter at room temperature plus butter for the pan
½	cup freshly grated Parmesan cheese
2	large eggs
1	cup buttermilk
2½	cups cake flour
¼	teaspoon salt
¾	teaspoon baking soda
¼	teaspoon freshly ground black pepper

Preheat the oven to 350°F. Butter an 8-inch cake pan.

In a mixing bowl, beat the butter and cheese together until smooth. Add the eggs and beat well. Stir in the buttermilk. Add the flour, salt, and baking soda and beat until smooth. Add the pepper and mix well.

Spoon the batter into the prepared pan and bake for about 25 minutes or until a cake tester inserted in the center comes out clean. Let rest in the pan for 5 minutes, then turn out on a wire rack to cool.

Best eaten the day it is made or may be frozen.

Butternut Croquettes

•

Winter Pot-au-Feu with Pureed Eggplant and Roasted Garlic

•

Parmesan Cake

•

Endive and Watercress Salad with Oranges and Fennel

•

Roast Apple Crème Brûlée with Gravenstein Cake

Wine suggestions: A medium-bodied California Merlot or an Italian Valpolicella

Savory Wine Biscuits

Originally developed as an alternative to the bland crackers often served with wine, these biscuits have the look and texture of thin biscotti. They are good plain or with just about any spread such as the Walnut and Roasted Red Pepper Pâté or the Lentil Puree with Olives, and Anchovies. This simple recipe comes from my friend Kathleen Orme, a partner in the Napa River Food Company in Napa, California.

WALNUT AND ROASTED RED

PEPPER PÂTÉ

•

SAVORY WINE BISCUITS

•

COLD CUCUMBER SOUP

WITH DILL

•

TENDER CORN CAKES WITH

GOAT CHEESE, WATERCRESS

SAUCE, AND SMOKED SALMON

•

PINEAPPLE CRUMBLE

WINE SUGGESTIONS:
A CALIFORNIA SÉMILLON OR A
DRY WHITE BORDEAUX

10 ounces St. Andre or similar triple-cream cheese,
softened to room temperature
¼   pound (1 stick) unsalted butter at room temperature
1   garlic clove, minced
2   cups all-purpose flour
¼   teaspoon salt

In a mixing bowl, thoroughly combine the cheese, butter, and garlic. Add the flour and salt and beat until smooth. Roll the dough into a cylinder 2 inches in diameter, wrap in plastic wrap, and refrigerate for 30 minutes or overnight.

Preheat the oven to 350°F.

Slice the dough into ⅛-inch-thick rounds and bake on an ungreased baking sheet for 8 to 10 minutes or until lightly brown at the edges. Cool on a wire rack. Stored in an airtight container, the Savory Wine Biscuits will keep for up to 1 week.

Sun-Dried Tomato and Gruyère Cheese Puffs

Makes 36 pieces

Serve these tasty mouthfuls either plain or split and stuffed (smoked trout makes a delectable filling). They can be made ahead and frozen; just reheat in a 350°F oven for 5 minutes or more. Vary the basic *pâté à choux* (cream puff paste) by omitting the tomatoes and substituting smoked Gouda for the Gruyère and rosemary for the thyme. This recipe comes from Kathleen Orme of Napa River Food Company.

1	cup water
¼	pound (1 stick) unsalted butter
⅛	teaspoon salt
1	cup sifted all-purpose flour
4	large eggs
¼	pound Gruyère cheese, grated
2	ounces oil-packed sun-dried tomatoes, drained and minced
¼	teaspoon dried thyme

Preheat the oven to 425°F.

In a saucepan, bring the water, butter, and salt to a boil. Add the flour all at once, stirring continuously until smooth. Remove from the heat and beat in the eggs one at a time. Stir in the cheese, tomatoes, and thyme.

Drop 1 tablespoon for each puff onto a cookie sheet lined with parchment paper and bake for 10 minutes; reduce the heat to 350°F and continue baking until golden, about 10 minutes more. Cool on a wire rack. Serve at once.

Sun-Dried Tomato and
Gruyère Cheese Puffs

•

Vegetarian Cassoulet

•

Mushroom Salad

•

Tuscan Fig and
Bread Tart

Wine suggestions:
A medium-bodied California
Zinfandel or a Chianti
Classico Riserva

Southern Persimmon Bread with Corn and Black Walnuts

MAKES TWO 9- BY 4½-INCH LOAVES

It would be reasonable to buy persimmons simply for the pleasure of taking them home and admiring them in a still life. From a culinary standpoint, however, these handsome native American fruits should be put to work in the kitchen, contributing deep glowing color and rich plummy taste to dishes both sweet and savory. The Indians of North America baked persimmons into their breads and puddings, so this recipe makes perfect sense as part of a Thanksgiving dinner. The bread is very good, too, for tea in the fall.

> **Butter or oil for the pans**
> 1 **cup coarsely chopped black walnuts**
> 1 **cup ripe Hachiya persimmon puree, skin and seeds discarded, from about 1 large persimmon**
> 1 **cup fresh or drained canned corn kernels**
> 3 **large eggs, lightly beaten**
> ⅔ **cup maple syrup**
> ⅔ **cup whole milk**
> ½ **cup vegetable oil**
> 2¼ **cups all-purpose flour, sifted**
> 1 **cup millet**
> 1 **tablespoon baking powder**
> 1 **teaspoon salt**

Preheat the oven to 350°F. Grease two 9- by 4½-inch loaf pans.

Toast the walnuts on a baking sheet for 10 minutes, turning them once.

In a medium mixing bowl, combine the persimmon puree, corn, eggs, maple syrup, milk, and vegetable oil and stir until well blended.

In another bowl, mix together the flour, millet, baking powder, and salt. Gradually add the dry ingredients to the wet ingredients, mixing completely after each addition. Stir in the walnuts. Do not overmix.

Pour the batter into the prepared pans and bake for about 1 hour or until a toothpick inserted into the center comes out clean. Cool the loaves in the pans for 10 minutes, then turn out on a wire rack. Let cool completely before slicing.

WINE SUGGESTIONS:
A FRUITY RED CÔTES-DU-RHÔNE OR A CALIFORNIA ZINFANDEL. IF YOU ARE SERVING THIS AROUND THANKSGIVING, TRY A NEWLY RELEASED BEAUJOLAIS NOUVEAU.

Catahoula's Cornmeal Waffles

MAKES 6 WAFFLES

Jan Birnbaum, chef/owner of Catahoula Restaurant and Saloon, in Calistoga, CA, came up with this winning recipe. He pairs them with the Catahoula's Tomatoes-in-All-Their-Glory Salad on page 179. They are delicious plain or smeared with fresh sheep's milk ricotta. Sometimes I add a jalapeño pepper, sometimes not.

½ **cup sifted cake flour**
¾ **cup cornmeal**
½ **tablespoon baking powder**
1 **teaspoon baking soda**
2 **tablespoons sugar**
  Pinch of salt
1 **fresh jalapeño pepper, seeded and minced, optional**
4 **large eggs, separated, at room temperature**
1 **cup buttermilk**
½ **cup milk**
1 **stick of unsalted butter, melted**
  Cooking spray or melted vegetable shortening

In a bowl, sift together the flour, cornmeal, baking powder, baking soda, sugar, and salt. Add the pepper if you are using it.

In a large mixing bowl, combine the egg yolks, buttermilk, milk, and butter, whisking until blended. Slowly add the dry ingredients to the wet ingredients. The batter will be quite thick.

Beat the egg whites until soft peaks form. Fold a third of the batter into the egg whites, then gently fold the egg whites into the batter. Do not overmix.

Heat the waffle iron, coat with cooking spray or brush with melted vegetable shortening. Pour in enough batter to just fill, about ½ cup per waffle. Close and bake until the steaming stops and the waffles are crisp, about 2 minutes. Cut in quarters and serve immediately. Delicious with the Catahoula's Tomatoes-in-All-Their-Glory Salad on page 179.

TOMATOES-IN-ALL-THEIR-
GLORY SALAD WITH
CORNMEAL WAFFLES

•

SALAD OF BLACK-EYED PEAS
AND VEGETABLES

•

ZUCCHINI CAKE WITH
FRUIT AND NUTS

WINE SUGGESTION:
A NICE FRUITY BEAUJOLAIS

Condiments

Chermoula

Mango Salsa

Pear Chutney with Red Peppers

Raita with Cucumbers and Radishes

Roasted Tomatillo and Avocado Sauce

Red Onion Marmalade

Walnut and Roasted Red Pepper Pâté

Watercress Salsa Verde

Tapenade

Lentil Puree with Olives and Anchovies

Orange-Scented Sun-Dried Tomato Relish

CHERMOULA

This is a streamlined California-style version of chermoula, Morocco's vibrant marinade for grilled and broiled fish. The constants of the traditional sauce are garlic, cumin, paprika, cilantro, and parsley. This variant leans heavily on parsley, lifted and lightened by fresh mint. It's wonderful swirled into soups or folded into grain and rice dishes.

4 **garlic cloves, minced**
1 **cup parsley leaves**
¼ **cup fresh mint leaves**
  Zest of 1 lemon
  Juice of ½ lemon
½ **cup extra-virgin olive oil**
  Salt to taste

Combine the garlic, parsley, mint, lemon zest, and juice in a blender and blend well. With the motor running, gradually add the oil in a steady, thin stream until the mixture is thick and emulsified. Season with salt. This is best used when made.

Variation: Substitute orange zest and juice for the lemon zest and juice and ½ cup basil for the parsley.

Mango Salsa

MAKES 6 CUPS

This is one of my favorite quick and healthful sauces, especially in spring and summer, when mangoes arrive in quantity from Mexico and Haiti.

2   ripe mangoes, peeled, seeded, and diced (about 2 cups)
2   red bell peppers, seeded and sliced into very thin, short
        julienne strips
1   small red onion, finely chopped
½   cup packed finely chopped cilantro leaves
1 to 2 garlic cloves to taste, minced
1   jalapeño chili, finely chopped
    Juice of 3 limes
¼   cup fresh orange juice

In a large nonreactive bowl, combine all the ingredients and gently mix together. Covered and refrigerated, the salsa will keep for 2 or 3 days.

CILANTRO MOUSSE

•

ASIAN SESAME

NOODLE SALAD

•

THAI-INSPIRED

SEAFOOD SALAD

•

MANGO SALSA

•

CARDAMOM SHORTBREAD

COOKIES

•

COCONUT ICE CREAM

WINE SUGGESTIONS:
A LIGHTER-BODIED BEER
OR AN OFF-DRY WHITE WINE
SUCH AS A CALIFORNIA
GEWÜRZTRAMINER WITH A
TOUCH OF SWEETNESS

How to Manage a Mango

Mangoes are notoriously messy to eat. "Share a mango in the bath with your loved one!" screams the old greengrocers' come-on for this most delicious of exotic fruits. The long, flat, irregularly shaped pit stubbornly resists separation from the orange flesh, and you may end up with a stew of liquidy pulp all over your hands if you don't attack with a plan in mind (never mind if you lose the battle—a mango is delectable in any condition).

For sliced mango, first peel the mango with a vegetable peeler, then cut the flesh lengthwise down to the pit in long parallel slices. Using the sharp tip of the knife, neatly cut individual slices away from the pit. Thin slices are easier to separate from the pit than thick ones.

To peel and dice a large-sized mango, try this technique: First stand the mango upright with the thin side toward you and slice down through it lengthwise in two parallel strokes, one on either side of the pit. You now have separated two unpeeled, boat-shaped sections from the pit. Score each of the two sections for dice, cutting down to (but not through) the skin. Next, invert the sections as though you were turning them inside out. You have now splayed the flesh of the mango. Cut close to the peel to free the cubes. Finally, peel the skin that's left on the mango, carve away the flesh clinging to the pit, and cut it in cubes.

PEAR CHUTNEY WITH RED PEPPERS

Slightly sweet and laced with unexpected heat, this fruit chutney is the perfect condiment for fall-weather dinners.

½ teaspoon hot red pepper flakes

1 tablespoon finely minced peeled fresh ginger
Zest of 1 orange

¼ teaspoon crushed cardamom seeds

1 2-inch piece of cinnamon stick

2 tablespoons unsalted butter

½ cup fresh orange juice

¼ cup firmly packed light brown sugar

6 medium Bosc pears, peeled, quartered, cored, and cut into ⅓-inch-thick slices

1 red bell pepper, seeded and cut into slivers 1 inch long and ⅛ inch wide

In a small mixing bowl, combine the red pepper flakes, ginger, orange zest, cardamom seeds, and cinnamon. Melt the butter in a large skillet over medium heat. Add the spices and fry for 1 to 2 minutes. Add the orange juice and sugar and stir over medium-high heat until the sugar is dissolved. Gently stir in the sliced pears and red pepper slivers. Bring to a simmer and cook, uncovered, for about 30 minutes, stirring occasionally at first, then more frequently during the last 10 minutes of cooking to prevent scorching.

Cool to room temperature. Serve or cover and refrigerate for up to 1 week.

GREEN BEANS WITH MUSTARD

SEEDS AND ALMONDS

•

SWEET POTATO PUREE WITH

AROMATIC SPICES

•

GINGERED SPINACH

WITH CILANTRO

•

RAITA WITH CUCUMBERS

AND RADISHES

•

PEAR CHUTNEY WITH

RED PEPPERS

WINE SUGGESTIONS:
BEER OR APPLE CIDER,
OR TRY A LOIRE SAVENNIÈRES
OR A LIGHT CALIFORNIA
CHENIN BLANC

Raita with Cucumbers and Radishes

MAKES 3 CUPS

In India raita is customarily made with cucumbers only, but I like to add radishes for their bright color and crunch. This is one of the most refreshing of dishes; it could easily take its place at the center of a light summer lunch, served along with the Green Beans with Mustard Seeds and Almonds.

- 2 medium cucumbers, partially peeled and sliced paper-thin, about 2 cups
- 1 teaspoon coarse salt
- 2 to 3 garlic cloves to taste
- 1½ cups plain yogurt or 1¼ cups yogurt and ¼ cup sour cream
- 2 tablespoons chopped fresh mint
- 1 teaspoon finely chopped lime zest
- 1 bunch of radishes, thinly sliced, about 1 cup
- 1 teaspoon black mustard seeds
- 2 teaspoons Asian sesame oil
- 1 mint leaf and 1 cucumber slice for garnish, optional

Sprinkle the cucumbers with half of the salt and leave in a colander to drain. Crush the garlic with the remaining salt; mix a few tablespoons of the yogurt with the garlic, then add the mixture to the rest of the yogurt and mix well. Add the mint, lime zest, and radishes.

Heat a small pan until hot but not smoking and in the dry pan fry the mustard seeds just until they pop and begin to turn gray, about 1 minute. Pat cucumbers dry. Fold them into the yogurt along with the mustard seeds and sesame oil and refrigerate until ready to serve. If you wish, decorate with a mint leaf and a twisted cucumber slice.

Roasted Tomatillo and Avocado Sauce

Makes about 2½ cups

The exotic-looking fruits of the tomatillo (*Physalis ixocarpa*) have pretty paper-lantern husks and look rather like primitive unripe tomatoes. They are available everywhere in California, but in supermarkets in other states you will most likely find them in the specialty produce section. They have a lemony-herbal tang and are quite delicious raw—try slicing them into salads. Charred in the oven or over an open flame, they add an extra dimension to whatever you blend with them. And of course they're the basis of *salsa verde*.

This sauce is great over just about anything or as a dip for corn chips. Try it with some breakfast ham and poached eggs for a spirited take on "green eggs and ham."

1	pound tomatillos, husked
1	small white onion
1 or 2	mild fresh chilies such as poblano or Anaheim to taste, taste before adding, both of these can be fiery
¾	cup tightly packed cilantro leaves
1	small to medium avocado, cubed
	Juice of 1 lime
1	teaspoon salt

Rinse the tomatillos and set aside a quarter of them.

In a large cast-iron skillet, dry-roast the tomatillos, unpeeled onion, and chilies over medium-high heat, shaking the pan frequently, until they are charred on all sides, about 15 minutes. Let the vegetables cool, then discard the onion skins and peel away any loose charred skin from the chilies and discard along with the stems and seeds.

In a food processor, puree the reserved tomatillos, the charred vegetables, the cilantro, and the avocado. Season with lime juice and salt.

Roasted Tomatillo and

Avocado Sauce

with Corn Chips

•

Mexican Hot and Sour

Soup with Hominy

•

Model Bakery

Corn-Chili Muffins

•

Hot-Sweet Coleslaw with

Caramelized Almonds

•

Banana-Colada Tart

Wine suggestions:

Medium-bodied beer or a

California Zinfandel with

forward fruit

Red Onion Marmalade

MAKES ABOUT 4 CUPS

A great spicy-sweet-tart condiment to have on hand. Excellent served with grilled seafood, chicken, or vegetables, it makes a tasty spread for pizza and adds life to sandwiches. You can whip it up on the spot, but I like to make it a day ahead to allow time for the flavors to develop.

¼   **cup olive oil**
8   **cups thinly sliced red onion, about 2 pounds**
1   **tablespoon grated fresh ginger**
3   **tablespoons light brown sugar**
1   **cup red wine vinegar**
¼   **teaspoon ground allspice**
    Salt to taste
4   **drops Tabasco sauce or to taste**

In a deep heavy skillet, heat the oil over low heat. Add the onion and cook, uncovered, until soft, moving the slices gently with a wooden spoon so as not to break them up. Add the remaining ingredients in the order listed and continue to simmer until the mixture has thickened, about 10 minutes more.

Cool to room temperature, cover, and refrigerate for several hours or overnight. Bring to room temperature before serving. This will keep for several days in the refrigerator.

WALNUT AND ROASTED RED PEPPER PÂTÉ

MAKES ABOUT 2 CUPS

The vivid flavors of this unusual spread are pleasantly hot and spicy. Use it on crackers or as a dip for crudités. Try a spoonful on grilled vegetables or fish.

2	medium red bell peppers
	olive oil to coat peppers, plus 2 teaspoons
¾	cup coarsely chopped walnuts
½	tablespoon cumin seeds
1	garlic clove, minced
2	teaspoons fresh lemon juice
	Harissa* to taste
¾ to 1 cup fresh bread crumbs, preferably from a good
	whole-grain loaf
	Salt and freshly ground black pepper to taste

Preheat the oven to 350°F.

Coat the peppers with olive oil and place on a baking sheet lined with foil. Roast for about 25 to 30 minutes until charred, turning several times to ensure even browning. Remove to a plastic or brown paper bag and let steam in the bag until cool to the touch. Peel the peppers over a bowl to catch any juices; discard the skins, seeds, and core.

Lightly toast the walnuts and cumin seeds in a nonstick skillet over medium heat for about 3 minutes, shaking the pan several times. Cool.

Using a mortar and pestle or a spice grinder, grind the walnuts and cumin seeds to a fine paste. Add the peppers and pound to a rough puree; add the garlic and puree again. Add the juices from the peppers, the lemon juice, and the 2 teaspoons olive oil. Add harissa to taste; the pâté will become hotter as it sits, so go easy.

Add enough bread crumbs to thicken the mixture slightly. Season with salt and pepper. Chill, covered, for at least 1 hour to allow the flavors to marry.

*Harissa is a fiery-hot chili-based paste of Tunisian origin. Very popular

WALNUT AND ROASTED RED
PEPPER PÂTÉ

•

SAVORY WINE BISCUITS

•

COLD CUCUMBER SOUP
WITH DILL

•

TENDER CORN CAKES WITH
GOAT CHEESE,
WATERCRESS SAUCE,
AND SMOKED SALMON

•

PINEAPPLE CRUMBLE

WINE SUGGESTIONS:
A CALIFORNIA SÉMILLON OR A
DRY WHITE BORDEAUX

throughout North Africa, it is usually set out on tables to accompany couscous, meat, and fish. With added oil it doubles as condiment, sauce, or marinade. Made fresh, it keeps for several weeks in the refrigerator, but for convenience you can buy some in a tube at a specialty food store or mail-order from Dean & Deluca (212-431-1691) or Adriana's Caravan (800-316-0820).

WATERCRESS SALSA VERDE

MAKES ABOUT 1½ CUPS

This piquant and peppery salsa is a fine accompaniment for grilled vegetables and broiled tomatoes. It goes especially well with grilled scallops and shrimp.

1   **large bunch of watercress, stems removed**
     Grated zest of 1 lemon
1   **tablespoon drained capers**
½   **cup cornichons**
½   **cup fruity olive oil**
     Salt and freshly ground black pepper to taste

Put all the ingredients in the bowl of a food processor or blender. Process or blend until the mixture is smooth. Serve at room temperature. Covered and refrigerated, the salsa will keep for several days.

GRILLED VINE LEAF PARCELS

•

EGGPLANT TORTE WITH FRESH

TOMATO COMPOTE

•

SAVORY BAKED RICOTTA

•

WATERCRESS SALSA VERDE

•

ZUCCHINI CAKE WITH

FRUIT AND NUTS

WINE SUGGESTIONS:
COTEAUX DU LANGUEDOC
OR A LIGHTER-BODIED
CALIFORNIA CABERNET
SAUVIGNON

Tapenade

MAKES 1½ CUPS

Straight from Provence, where summer cooking explodes with lusty tastes and smells, this superuseful "poor man's caviar" is traditionally spread on crackers and served with anise-flavored pastis. Though named for the capers it contains, tapenade is an olive-based paste. Try it as a garnish for fresh tomatoes or deviled eggs; use some as a flavor enhancer for grilled vegetables or chicken; toss it with fresh pasta.

This version combines assertively flavored, deep purple olives with peppery, pale green olives from Sicily.

½   cup good-quality salt-cured black olives, pitted
¼   cup imported Sicilian (green) olives, pitted
3   anchovy fillets, rinsed and drained on a paper towel
1   garlic clove, peeled
2   tablespoons capers, preferably salt-packed, rinsed and drained
1   tablespoon fresh lemon juice
¼   cup fruity olive oil
     Freshly ground black pepper to taste

In a blender or a food processor, combine the olives, anchovies, garlic, capers, and lemon juice. Blend or process until smooth.

With the motor running, add the olive oil little by little to make a thick sauce as you would for a mayonnaise. Add a few grinds of pepper to taste. Stored in an airtight container in the refrigerator, the tapenade will keep for about 1 week.

LENTIL PUREE WITH OLIVES AND ANCHOVIES

An intensely flavored variation on tapenade that I use again and again. This dark, rich puree from the south of France makes an unusual dip for raw vegetables, is delicious spread on crostini, complements the taste of grilled fish, and even works well rolled up in thinly sliced prosciutto.

1   cup dried green or brown lentils, picked over
½   cup pitted oil-cured olives, green or black
5   anchovy fillets, rinsed and drained on a paper towel
1   vine-ripened tomato, peeled, and seeded
2   large garlic cloves, coarsely chopped
    Juice and zest of 1 lemon
¼   teaspoon hot red pepper flakes
¾   cup extra-virgin olive oil
    Salt to taste
2   tablespoons minced fresh mint

Cook the lentils according to the package directions until very tender. Do not drain them. Cool.

In a food processor, puree the cooled lentils along with the remaining ingredients except the olive oil, salt, and mint. With the motor running, add the olive oil through the feeding tube in a steady stream and process until the mixture is smooth and creamy. Add salt if needed. Garnish with fresh mint just before serving.

The Lentil Puree can be stored in the refrigerator for several days but should be brought to room temperature before it is used.

LENTIL PUREE WITH OLIVES
AND ANCHOVIES

•

MINESTRONE WITH
ROSEMARY-CHILI PESTO

•

FENNEL AND ASIAGO TWISTS

•

PINEAPPLE CRUMBLE

WINE SUGGESTIONS:
A MEDIUM-BODIED ZINFANDEL
OR A CHÂTEAUNEUF-DU-PAPE

ORANGE-SCENTED SUN-DRIED TOMATO RELISH

MAKES ABOUT 4 CUPS

This relish is delicious over grilled fish or chicken or tossed with pasta. No cheese, please.

¼   cup dry white wine
¼   cup red wine vinegar
¼   cup sugar
1   tablespoon olive oil
2   tablespoons finely diced red onion
2   tablespoons finely diced yellow or red bell pepper
1½ cups chopped seeded ripe tomatoes
½   cup sun-dried tomatoes in oil, drained well, patted dry, and thinly sliced
½   cup tomato juice
1   teaspoon grated orange zest
4   oranges, separated into segments with all white pith removed
    Salt and cayenne pepper to taste

In a small saucepan, simmer the wine, vinegar, and sugar over high heat until syrupy and reduced to about ¼ cup. Remove from the heat and cool.

Heat the oil in a small skillet over medium heat. Sauté the onion and bell pepper in it until just crisp-tender, about 6 minutes. Cool slightly.

In a bowl, combine all the ingredients. Cover and let stand at room temperature for about 2 hours to allow the flavors to blend. The relish will keep, covered, in the refrigerator for up to 3 days.

Note: For a lovely variation, use kumquats in place of the oranges. Omit the orange segments and grated orange zest. Thinly slice 1 pound of kumquats, then simmer them along with the wine, vinegar, and sugar until the liquid is reduced to about ¼ cup.

Desserts

Perfect Gingerbread

Maple Pears with Cardamom Cream

Roast Apple Crème Brûlée with Gravenstein Cake

Apricot Spoon Bread

Banana-Colada Tart

Cardamom Shortbread Cookies

Figs in Armagnac

Mangoes in Gin with Coconut Ice Cream

Modeste aux Cerises

Orange-Yogurt Cornmeal Cake

Pears Baked in Cream

Pineapple Crumble

Strawberries in Lemon Verbena with Fresh Cheese Ice Cream

Chocolate Pudding Cake

Couscous Pudding with Pineapple and Strawberries

Tuscan Fig and Bread Tart

Black Sesame Tuiles

Zucchini Cake with Fruit and Nuts

Lavender Shortbreads

Peach and Blueberry Buckle

Rhubarb Cobbler

Fruit with Wine

    Melon with Port

    A Raisin Nightcap

Perfect Gingerbread

Living in a land of to-die-for local figs, exotic Meyer lemons, and ambrosial late-harvest dessert wines nuanced with dozens of honeyed flavor notes, I still find myself hankering after a finale of good old-fashioned gingerbread once the weather cools down. A really good gingerbread is hard to find, so I'm forever searching down new versions, to fill the house with their enticing aroma. This recipe featuring fresh ginger and cayenne pepper is my current favorite. For an elegant companion, serve this with the Maple Pears with Cardamom Cream.

Butter and flour for the pan
1½   **cups sifted cake flour**
1   **teaspoon baking powder**
1   **teaspoon ground cinnamon**
¼   **teaspoon salt**
⅛   **teaspoon cayenne pepper**
½   **cup unsalted butter at room temperature**
¼   **cup dark molasses**
¼   **cup honey**
2   **teaspoons peeled and finely grated fresh ginger**
½   **cup water**
½   **cup packed light brown sugar**
1   **large egg, lightly beaten**
2   **teaspoons grated lemon zest, from 1 lemon**

Preheat the oven to 350°F. Butter a 9-inch-square baking pan and line the bottom with a sheet of buttered wax or parchment paper. Dust with flour.

Sift together the cake flour, baking powder, cinnamon, salt, and cayenne.

Place the butter, molasses, honey, ginger, and water in a large microwave-safe bowl. Place the bowl, covered, in the microwave and cook on high power for 2 to 3 minutes or until the butter is melted. Remove and set aside. (You can also simmer the mixture on the stove in a double boiler until the butter is melted.)

In a separate bowl, whisk together the brown sugar, egg, and lemon zest. Whisk this mixture, bit by bit, into the butter-molasses mixture. Gradually whisk in the dry ingredients until you have a smooth batter. Pour into the prepared pan.

Bake for 35 minutes, covering with foil for the last 10 minutes. The gingerbread is done when a toothpick inserted into the center comes out clean. Let rest in the pan for 10 minutes before unmolding onto a wire rack. Best served warm.

MAPLE PEARS WITH CARDAMOM CREAM

SERVES 12

A gift-of-the-gods autumn dessert.

Aristocrats of their tribe and the greatest of all pears for eating out of hand, chubby Comice pears are unequaled for their succulence and buttery texture. Search them out in fall and early winter in fruit markets and specialty food stores. Just-ripe Bartletts work perfectly well if you can't get the creamy Comice.

1	cup crème fraîche or sweetened yogurt
½	teaspoon ground cardamom
6	Comice pears, peeled, quartered, and cored
	Juice of 1 lemon
2	tablespoons unsalted butter
2	tablespoons pure maple syrup

In a chilled mixing bowl, beat the crème fraîche until smooth. Add the cardamom, cover, and refrigerate for 15 minutes or until ready to serve.

Sprinkle the pears with lemon juice.

Melt the butter in a large deep saucepan or casserole over medium-high heat. Add the pears and cook, stirring frequently, uncovered, until the pears begin to brown and are tender when pierced with a fork, about 15 to 20 minutes. Add the maple syrup and cook for several minutes more.

Briefly whisk together the chilled cream until it's thick. Serve the pears warm or at room temperature topped with the cream.

ROAST APPLE CRÈME BRÛLÉE WITH GRAVENSTEIN CAKE

SERVES 8

Jerry Comfort, executive chef at Beringer Vineyards in Napa Valley, created this delectable fall dessert. It has an unusual twist: the cake is crumbled just before serving. If you like, you can prepare this in easy stages over a 3-day period. Bake the apples up to 2 days in advance; fill and bake with the custard 1 day ahead. You can make the cake anytime and freeze it; bring it to room temperature before crumbling. The cake is great on its own, uncrumbled, with a dollop of sweetened whipped cream.

Sweet-tart and juicy Gravensteins are an early-crop apple grown primarily on the West Coast.

8   small baking apples
1   cup apple cider
1   cup heavy cream
2   large eggs, lightly beaten
½   cup plus 4 teaspoons sugar
½   teaspoon vanilla extract
    Confectioners' sugar

Gravenstein Cake

3   cups all-purpose flour
1   tablespoon baking soda
1   tablespoon ground cinnamon
1½   teaspoons baking powder
1½   teaspoons salt
6   cups coarsely grated Gravenstein or other good
     cooking apples such as Jonathan, Winesap, or Granny
     Smith, about 4 pounds
3   large eggs, lightly beaten
2¼   cups packed light brown sugar
1½   cups chopped walnuts
¾   cup canola oil
     Butter for the baking dish

BUTTERNUT CROQUETTES

•

WINTER POT-AU-FEU WITH
PUREED EGGPLANT AND
ROASTED GARLIC

•

PARMESAN CAKE

•

ENDIVE AND WATERCRESS
SALAD WITH ORANGES
AND FENNEL

•

ROAST APPLE CRÈME BRÛLÉE
WITH GRAVENSTEIN CAKE

WINE SUGGESTIONS:
A MEDIUM-BODIED
CALIFORNIA MERLOT OR A
FULLER PINOT NOIR

Preheat the oven to 400°F.

Use a melon baller to scoop out the core and seeds of each apple. Do not pierce the skin. Fill each apple with ⅛ cup cider and place in a baking pan. Add water to a depth of 2 inches. Bake for approximately 35 to 40 minutes or until cooked through. Discard the cider and water from the pan and set the apples aside to cool.

Combine the cream, eggs, ½ cup sugar, and vanilla in a mixing bowl. Pour through a fine-mesh strainer. Return the cooled apples to the baking pan and fill with the custard; surround with water to a depth of 2 inches. Reduce the oven temperature to 325°F and bake for approximately 45 minutes. Remove from the water and cool.

For the cake, preheat the oven to 350°F.

In a large bowl, sift together the first 5 cake ingredients. Set aside.

In a separate bowl, combine the grated apples, eggs, brown sugar, walnuts, and oil. Add the sifted dry ingredients and mix until just blended. Spread the batter in a greased 9- by 13-inch baking dish. Bake for 1 hour or until a toothpick inserted in the center comes out clean. Cool in the pan for 10 minutes, then remove to a wire rack until completely cooled.

To serve, crumble the cake and dust individual dessert plates with confectioners' sugar. Place about ½ cup of the crumbled cake in the center of each plate. Preheat the broiler. Trim about ¼ inch off the top of each apple so that each has a nice flat surface. Place the apples on a baking sheet. Sprinkle about ½ teaspoon sugar over the top of each custard-filled apple. Place the baking sheet under the broiler as close as possible to the heat and caramelize tops of the apples until golden to dark brown; watch carefully. Place one apple in the center of each cake nest and serve at once.

APRICOT SPOON BREAD

SERVES 8

Contrary to popular assumption and most cookbooks, spoon bread is not a bread at all but the light and delicate southern cornmeal cousin of the French soufflé. Slightly sweetened and flavored with ground almonds, it makes a delicious topping for cooked fruit. Don't expect it to puff up as much as a real soufflé. Spoon bread is best eaten warm right from the oven, while it's still puffy and light. Any leftovers are great for breakfast the next morning.

Almost every apricot I have ever bought in a market has been mealy and flat tasting (see page 231). This simple spoon bread is a good way to use the less-than-perfect ones. This recipe is every bit as good made with green-gage plums in the fall.

DOUBLE CELERY SOUP WITH
APPLE AND DILL

•

COD BAKED IN PARCHMENT
WITH CHERMOULA-COUSCOUS
CRUST

•

ORANGE-SCENTED SUN-DRIED
TOMATO RELISH

•

GINGERED SPINACH WITH
CILANTRO

•

APRICOT SPOON BREAD

WINE SUGGESTION:
A FULL-BODIED PINOT NOIR

3	tablespoons unsalted butter
2¼	cups water
⅔	cup stone-ground cornmeal
1	teaspoon salt
4	large eggs, beaten
¼	cup sugar
⅓	cup ground almonds
1	cup buttermilk
⅛	teaspoon almond extract
2½	pounds ripe fresh apricots, cut in half and pitted
1	vanilla bean, seeds scraped and pod finely chopped
½	teaspoon grated lemon zest
⅓	cup sugar

Preheat the oven to 400°F. Butter a 3-quart ovenproof casserole with 1 tablespoon of the butter.

Bring 2 cups of the water to a boil, add the cornmeal and salt in a steady stream, and cook, stirring, for 1 minute. Beat in the remaining butter, eggs, ¼ cup sugar, nuts, buttermilk, and almond extract until smooth.

In a nonreactive saucepan, combine the apricots, vanilla bean and seeds, lemon zest, and ⅓ cup additional sugar and remaining water. Cover and cook slowly over low heat, stirring occasionally until tender, about 10 minutes.

Pour the apricot mixture into the buttered casserole, spread the spoon bread mixture on top, and bake for 40 minutes or until a tester inserted in the center comes out clean. Serve at once, or it will fall.

Apricots—Fresh or Dried

Like many early fruits, apricots have a brief season, from late May through July. The in-season apricots you buy in markets may look the part, but unless you live in the West you may be disappointed in their quality. Apricots sold east of the Rockies are picked unripened in California, where almost the entire domestic crop is grown, so that they will survive long-distance shipping. These apricots will inevitably lack the luscious tangy sweetness and rich perfume of tree-ripened fruit. (Once picked, their sugar content does not increase.) However, they are quite acceptable when cooked in recipes both savory and sweet—even jam—to concentrate their flavor.

Sometimes high-quality, naturally dried apricots plumped in liquid overnight are a better choice than mishandled hard or mushy fresh fruit. The aroma and flavor of the sulfur dioxide used as a preservative in most dried fruit is particularly noticeable in dried apricots. Soaking the fruit in boiling water for a minute or two may reduce the odor, but if you find the sulfur unpleasant or if you are allergic to sulfides, you can find sulfur-free, organically grown dried apricots in natural foods stores or mail-order them from Timber Crest Farms (4791 Dry Creek Road, Healdsburg, CA 95448; 707-433-8251). Store sulfur-free fruit in the refrigerator. The sumptuous taste of apricots is too good to pass up just because you live east of Denver.

If you find some fresh apricots of deep golden-amber flushed rose or, best of all, you have ripe fruit straight from the tree, enjoy them on their own with a little yogurt or crème fraîche or serve them with Gorgonzola, Roquefort, or Camembert cheese and some walnuts or pistachios.

Banana-Colada Tart

Sweetened condensed milk is commonly used in dessert recipes originating in the tropics, where refrigeration was formerly unavailable. Adding coconut and banana to traditional key lime pie filling gives this old favorite a new look and a bit of sophistication.

Note: Key limes are not grown commercially though they sometimes appear in supermarkets in late winter. You can use regular limes or try Nellie and Joe's Key West Lime Juice, an acceptable substitute for the real thing (call 800-LIMEPIE for your nearest retailer).

- 1½ cups sweetened shredded coconut
- 1½ cups wheatmeal or graham crackers, crumbled
- ½ cup confectioners' sugar
- 10 tablespoons unsalted butter, cut into small pieces
- 6 large egg yolks
- 2 14-ounce cans sweetened condensed milk
- 2 ripe bananas, mashed
- 2 limes, zest only, minced
- 1 cup lime juice, (about 4 to 5 limes)
  Fresh strawberries and confectioners' sugar for garnish, optional

Preheat the oven to 350°F.

Spread the coconut on a baking sheet and toast in the oven until golden brown, about 3 to 4 minutes, tossing every few minutes. Watch carefully. Cool on the baking sheet.

Combine the cracker crumbs, sugar, and half the toasted coconut in a mixing bowl or food processor. Add the butter a little at a time and process or mix by hand until the mixture resembles oatmeal. Pat this dough into a 9- by 13-inch baking dish. Bake for 20 minutes. Cool on a rack.

Beat together the egg yolks, condensed milk, and banana until thick. Add the lime zest and juice. Spread the filling over the prebaked crust. Sprinkle with the remaining coconut. Bake for 8 to 10 minutes or until set. Cool completely on a rack, then chill in the refrigerator until ready to

TIERRA FARMS

BLACK BEAN CHILI

•

MODEL BAKERY

CORN-CHILI MUFFINS

•

JÍCAMA AND TOASTED PUMPKIN

SEED SALAD WITH ORANGE-

GARLIC VINAIGRETTE

•

BANANA-COLADA TART

WINE SUGGESTIONS:
BEER, PREFERABLY AN AMBER
BEER SERVED WITH WEDGES OF
LIME, WOULD BE BEST WITH THIS
MENU. OR TRY A YOUNG
ZINFANDEL OR
AUSTRALIAN SHIRAZ.

serve. (The tart is also delicious served slightly frozen.) Decorate each serving with fresh strawberries if desired and a dusting of confectioners' sugar.

CARDAMOM SHORTBREAD COOKIES

MAKES 24

Warmly fragranced, earthy cardamom is an important spice in Indian sweets. These cookies are delicious with fresh fruit.

1½ cups unsalted butter at room temperature
1   teaspoon crushed cardamom seeds
½   cup firmly packed light brown sugar
2½ cups all-purpose flour
½   cup stone-ground cornmeal
¼   teaspoon salt
¼   teaspoon baking powder
    Confectioners' sugar for dusting, optional

Preheat the oven to 325°F.

In a large mixing bowl, cream together the butter and cardamom. Gradually add the brown sugar and beat until light and fluffy.

In a small mixing bowl, combine the flour, cornmeal, salt, and baking powder. Add these dry ingredients to the butter mixture, beating with an electric mixer or by hand until thoroughly incorporated.

Press the dough into an ungreased 8- by 10-inch baking pan. Score the top with a knife to outline 24 cookies and prick the surface of each one in 3 places with the tines of a lightly floured fork. Bake for 1 hour or until pale golden in color; do not brown. Cool for 10 minutes in the pan. Carefully cut the shortbread on the scored markings and remove the cookies to a wire rack to cool completely. Dust with confectioners' sugar just before serving if you wish. Store in an airtight container.

FIGS IN ARMAGNAC

SERVES 4

The soul of simplicity, perfect after a rich meal.

½ **pound dried figs, preferably the small thick-skinned Kadota**
½ **cup Armagnac or late-harvest Riesling, Gewürztraminer, or Sémillon**
1 **tablespoon grated orange zest**

Cut the figs in half and put them in a nonreactive serving bowl with the liqueur and orange zest. Cover and let soak for at least 30 minutes.

TOMATO ASPIC WITH SAFFRON-

HERB MAYONNAISE

•

SEA BASS BAKED

ON A BED OF ARTICHOKES,

ASPARAGUS, AND SHALLOTS

•

MASHED POTATOES WITH LEEKS

•

CARDAMOM SHORTBREAD

COOKIES

•

FIGS IN ARMAGNAC

WINE SUGGESTIONS:
A CRISP CALIFORNIA
CHARDONNAY OR AN ITALIAN
CORTESE DI GAVI

Mangoes in Gin with Coconut Ice Cream

This divine fruit with its tropical color and flavor is paired perfectly with coconut ice cream.

Wine suggestions:
An Alsatian Pinot Blanc or
an off-dry
California Riesling

2 **large ripe mangoes, peeled and sliced into strips**
2 **limes, juice only**
2 **tablespoons gin**
   Coconut Ice Cream (recipe follows)

In a shallow nonreactive dish, arrange the mango slices in a single layer, add the lime juice and gin, cover, and macerate for 30 minutes in the refrigerator.

To serve, place several mango slices in a dessert bowl and spoon some of the juices over them. Add a scoop of Coconut Ice Cream. If you want a cookie too, serve the Cardamom Shortbread Cookies or the Black Sesame Tuiles.

Coconut Ice Cream

MAKES 1 QUART

1 **14-ounce can unsweetened coconut milk, available at Asian and Indian markets or gourmet sections of supermarkets**
6 **large egg yolks**
1½ **cups whipping cream, milk, or half-and-half**
1 **teaspoon vanilla or almond extract**

In a nonreactive saucepan, heat the coconut milk, whisk in the egg yolks, and cook over low heat, stirring constantly, until the mixture coats a spoon. Strain into a container and stir in the cream or milk and the vanilla or almond extract. Pour into an ice cream maker and freeze according to the manufacturer's instructions.

This is best made a day ahead, then put into a container to harden in the freezer.

MODESTE AUX CERISES

This simple cherry tart from Provence makes a deliciously simple rustic dessert. Similar to a clafouti in spirit, but crunchier.

1   tablespoon unsalted butter
3 to 4 tablespoons sugar as needed
1½   pounds fresh sweet cherries, pitted
¼   cup whole blanched almonds
2   tablespoons all-purpose flour
⅓   cup confectioners' sugar plus a little for dusting
2   extra-large egg whites at room temperature
      Pinch of cream of tartar

Preheat the oven to 325°F. Butter a 10-inch round gratin dish or a 9- by 13- by 2-inch-deep baking dish. Sprinkle with 1 tablespoon of the sugar.

Arrange the cherries over the bottom of the dish in a single layer; sprinkle with 1 to 2 tablespoons of the sugar, depending on the sweetness of the cherries.

In a food processor, grind together the almonds, flour, and ⅓ cup confectioners' sugar until fine in texture.

Beat the egg whites with the cream of tartar until soft peaks form. Beat in the remaining tablespoon of sugar. Continue beating until stiff but not dry. Gently fold half of the whites into the flour/nut mixture, then fold in the remaining whites. Gently spread the mixture over the cherries and bake for 40 to 45 minutes or until the topping is dry. Serve warm or at room temperature, dusted with confectioners' sugar.

BOUILLABAISSE OF FENNEL

AND POTATO

•

STUFFED ARTICHOKES

•

MIXED GREENS WITH

TAPENADE VINAIGRETTE

•

MODESTE AUX CERISES

WINE SUGGESTIONS:

A CRISP, DRY CALIFORNIA

SAUVIGNON BLANC OR A

FRENCH BEAUJOLAIS OR

ITALIAN BARBERA D'ALBA

How to Pit a Cherry

Buy one of the simple gadgets made for this purpose available at most cookware stores. A cherry stoner won't cost you very much, and you can also use it to pit olives and beach plums. One device works on the principle of spring-release pliers: fruit is placed in a small ring and, as the jaws close, a punch goes through it and the pit drops out. If you have a serious taste for cherry pie, you might want to invest in a deluxe stoner, an automatic model with spring-loaded plunger and large feeder funnel that can pit a pound of cherries in little more than a minute (about $40 from *The Chef's Catalog* 3245 Commercial Avenue, Northbrook, IL 60062; 800-338-3232).

Other, homelier methods include pulling out the stem and pinching the cherry to push the cherrystone through the stem hole or extracting the stone with a small knife or even a paper clip. The juice stains, so you may want to take the work outside to a quiet corner away from curious bees.

Cherries Sweet and Sour

Cherries are the first orchard fruit of the year. They don't last long in markets, as fugitive as those two other spring glories—asparagus and strawberries. Our leading commercial variety is the beautiful sweet Bing cherry, dark glossy red and juicy. The red Lambert, the Van, the yellow, red-blushed Royal Ann (or Napoleon) and the golden Rainier (expensive but supersweet) are other sweet cherries sold fresh in the United States.

More complex flavors are evident in the sour cherries, the dark red Morello and the lighter Montmorency—but you are lucky if you find some. Vastly superior for cooking, these cherries of character are rarely found in U.S. markets because almost the whole crop is spirited away for canning and freezing. Look for Duke cherries, including Olivet, Reine Hortense, and Royal Duke, which are crosses between the sweet and sour strains. Dried and pitted tart Morello cherries from Michigan are available for a price in gourmet shops; American Spoon Foods of Petoskey is a widely distributed brand and an excellent mail-order source (1668 Clarion Avenue, Petoskey, MI 49770; 800-222-5886). A delicious (though costly) snack food, dried cherries can be substituted for or combined with raisins in cooking or, softened in a little red wine, added for tang to savory sauces.

ORANGE-YOGURT CORNMEAL CAKE

Satisfy your sweet tooth with this low-fat version of an orange-yogurt cake from Greece. For a fanciful presentation, encircle the cake with orange segments, small whole strawberries, and tiny sprigs of fresh mint.

WINE SUGGESTIONS:
A GIGONDAS OR A
MEDIUM-BODIED CALIFORNIA
RHÔNE BLEND

Vegetable oil spray
1½ **cups uncooked cream of wheat**
1½ **cups stone-ground yellow cornmeal**
½   **cup all-purpose flour**
2   **teaspoons baking powder**
1   **teaspoon baking soda**
2   **cups nonfat plain yogurt**
½   **cup finely ground almonds**
¼   **cup frozen orange juice concentrate**
1   **tablespoon grated orange zest**
1   **cup dark honey**
    Confectioners' sugar

Preheat the oven to 350°F. Coat a 10-inch nonstick bundt pan with vegetable oil spray.

In a mixing bowl, sift together the cream of wheat, cornmeal, flour, baking powder, and soda. Make a well in the center of the dry ingredients and add the yogurt, almonds, orange juice concentrate, orange zest, and honey. Stir well.

Pour the batter into the prepared pan and bake until the top is golden, about 45 minutes. Cool in the pan for 10 minutes, then remove and cool on a wire rack.

Wrapped well in plastic wrap or foil, the cake will keep moist for several days. It also can be frozen. Sprinkle the cake with confectioners' sugar just before serving.

PEARS BAKED IN CREAM

Fragrant cooked pears are a favorite of mine after a rich main course. Baked or poached, they have an effortless elegance, classic in its simplicity. (Even easier to prepare and marked by the same note of refinement are succulent ripe pears in season served along with some rich blue-veined cheese and a few cracked walnuts.)

	Butter for the pan
3	**large slightly underripe pears, peeled**
2	**teaspoons water**
2	**tablespoons sugar**
1	**cup heavy cream**
2	**tablespoons finely chopped pistachios**

Preheat the oven to 350°F. Butter a 9- by 13-inch baking dish.

Cut the pears in half, core, and thinly slice, keeping halves intact. Arrange the pears in the dish, slightly fanning out the slices. Sprinkle with the water and sugar and bake for 20 minutes. Pour on the heavy cream and continue cooking for 15 to 20 more minutes. To serve, place one pear half on each plate and sprinkle with the chopped pistachios.

WILD RICE PANCAKES

•

STIR-FRIED ASIAN GREENS

•

TANGY GREENS AND
WHEATBERRY SOUP

•

PEARS BAKED IN CREAM

WINE SUGGESTIONS:
FRUITY GERMAN
MÜLLER-THURGAU OR
AN OFF-DRY
CALIFORNIA RIESLING

❧ Sorting Out the Pears for Cooking ❧

Although Bartletts are available all year and are fine for cooking if used a shade underripe, even the most underwhelming of produce aisles will generally stock some preferable alternatives: tall, shapely rock-hard Boscs or small rock-hard Seckels or green rock-hard Anjous, or Comice, all of which will, once you get them home, turn creamy soft, sweet, juicy, and perfumed in a matter of days—perfect for baking or poaching since their flesh stays firm when cooked and their skins neither pucker nor crack.

Harder to find but well worth seeking out are these firm-fleshed, late-season pears for cooking: Honeysweet, bite-size and juicy, like a russet Seckel; ball-shaped Dumont, a late-ripening, excellent keeper; Forelle, the stippled "trout pear," sweet and juicy; the handsome Red Bartlett, with flavor identical to the yellow; Rogue Red, tasting like a caramel apple (look for it in the South); and Winter Nelis, creamy, winey, aromatic—a first-class baking pear.

PINEAPPLE CRUMBLE

SERVES 8

Lovers of good old-fashioned pineapple upside-down cake will love this dessert. It's a lot simpler to make, too.

Butter for the baking dish
2   **medium pineapples, peeled, cored, and sliced into 1-inch cubes, about 6 to 8 cups**
1   **cup packed dark brown sugar**
1   **teaspoon ground cinnamon**
    Pinch of freshly grated nutmeg
½   **cup Myers's dark rum**

The Topping

1   **cup all-purpose flour**
1   **cup quick-cooking rolled oats**
½   **cup packed light brown sugar**
½   **teaspoon salt**
½   **teaspoon freshly grated nutmeg**
1   **large egg, beaten**
¼   **cup vegetable oil**

Preheat the oven to 350°F. Grease a 9- by 13-inch baking dish with butter.

Arrange the pineapple in one layer in the baking dish. In a small mixing bowl, combine the brown sugar, cinnamon, and nutmeg. Sprinkle over the pineapple. Pour the rum into the baking dish.

To make the topping, combine the flour, oats, light brown sugar, salt, and nutmeg in a large bowl. Stir in the egg and then the oil, blending until the mixture is moist and crumbly.

Sprinkle the oat mixture evenly over the pineapple to cover (do not press or pack it down). Bake for 40 minutes or until golden brown on top. This is delicious served with a small scoop of vanilla ice cream—but what isn't?

WALNUT AND ROASTED

RED PEPPER PÂTÉ

•

SAVORY WINE BISCUITS

•

COLD CUCUMBER SOUP

WITH DILL

•

TENDER CORN CAKES WITH

GOAT CHEESE, WATERCRESS

SAUCE, AND SMOKED SALMON

•

PINEAPPLE CRUMBLE

WINE SUGGESTIONS:

A CALIFORNIA SÉMILLON OR A

DRY WHITE BORDEAUX

Strawberries in Lemon Verbena with Fresh Cheese Ice Cream

SERVES 8

This is a favorite dish at the beautifully restored Hôtel de La Mirande in Avignon, directly across from the Papal Palace. The Cheese Ice Cream tastes not at all cheesy but more like slightly sweetened frozen crème fraîche or sour cream. The syrup should be prepared at least an hour before serving.

Cheese Ice Cream

½   pound mascarpone cheese
½   cup clover or lavender honey
2   teaspoons fresh lemon juice
½   cup heavy cream

Lemon Verbena Syrup

¼   cup fresh lemon verbena, lemon balm, or lemon thyme
    leaves
2   cups sugar
⅔   cup water

4   cups strawberries, hulled and cut in half if large
½   cup tightly packed fresh mint leaves, rinsed, dried, and
    cut into a chiffonade

In a medium bowl, blend together the ice cream ingredients in the order listed until smooth. Pour this mixture into an ice cream maker and freeze according to the manufacturer's instructions. Transfer the frozen ice cream to a clean container, cover, and place in the freezer until ready to serve.

For the syrup, mix the verbena leaves with the sugar in a blender and blend until fine in texture.

In a 3-quart saucepan, bring the water to a boil. Add the sugar-verbena mixture and return to the boil. Remove from the heat. If you wish, strain the syrup through a fine-mesh strainer after 5 minutes to remove the verbena leaves.

To serve, place ½ cup strawberries into each of 8 dessert bowls. Pour some of the syrup over the berries while it is still a little warm. Add a scoop of the ice cream and decorate with mint.

Note: To make a chiffonade, begin by stacking leaves, placing the largest at the bottom. Tightly roll up the stacks of leaves lengthwise. Cut across the roll to produce thin ribbons, or chiffonade.

CHOCOLATE PUDDING CAKE

SERVES 6

A fifties favorite revisited. Certain desserts come and go in popularity, and pudding cakes, at once sophisticated and consoling, are today enjoying a revival. During baking the batter obligingly separates into cake and pudding before the light and puffy result is inverted and served upside down on your plate. The version most of us remember was flavored with lemon, but for me the best one of all is warm, creamy, crunchy—and made with chocolate. The pleasure is intensified when a dollop of vanilla ice cream accompanies the warm cake.

7	ounces bittersweet chocolate, broken into small bite-size pieces
¼	pound (1 stick) unsalted butter
4	large eggs, separated, at room temperature
1	teaspoon vanilla extract
1	cup sugar
½	cup all-purpose flour
½	teaspoon baking powder
	Pinch of salt
	Confectioners' sugar for dusting top

Preheat the oven to 350°F. Lightly butter six 4½-ounce ramekins or custard cups.

Melt 4 ounces of the chocolate with the butter in a double boiler or in the microwave. Cool. Add the egg yolks, vanilla, and sugar and beat until smooth.

Sift together the flour, baking powder, salt, and fold them into the chocolate mixture. Beat the egg whites until stiff but not dry and fold them into the mixture.

Spoon the batter into the custard cups, filling each almost to the rim. Bury the remaining pieces of chocolate in the custard cups, about 3 pieces per cup. Place the cups in a baking pan and set the pan on an oven rack. Fill the pan with enough boiling water to come halfway up the sides of the cups. Bake for 25 to 30 minutes or until the cake rises above the rims of the cups by about 1 inch; the surface should look slightly cracked. Let stand for 5 minutes in the pan. Invert onto serving plates and dust with confectioners' sugar or serve in the custard cup.

You can make the pudding cakes ahead of time and reheat them in their cups in the microwave for 1 minute on high power or in a preheated 350°F oven for about 10 minutes. The idea is to soften the pudding on the bottom before unmolding.

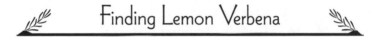

Finding Lemon Verbena

Only fresh leaves of this herb will do. To have them you must buy lemon verbena (*Aloysia triphylla*) in the spring in the herb section of a good nursery. Once planted in a sunny location, three or four of the little plants should give you plenty of lemon scented leaves to put in teas and coolers, add to ripe summer fruits, and decorate dishes both savory and sweet. If you live in a climate they favor (native to South America, they have made themselves at home around the Mediterranean, where their exhilarating lemony fragrance distinguishes many soaps and cosmetics), you can enjoy them all year long.

Lemon balm (*Melissa officinalis*) and lemon thyme (*Thymus citriodora*) are acceptable substitutes if you can't find the real thing.

COUSCOUS PUDDING WITH PINEAPPLE AND STRAWBERRIES

SERVES 6

This is a lovely light not-too-sweet dessert for spring, when the strawberries start to come in. You may substitute rhubarb for the pineapple, but add a little extra sugar if you do and make sure you cook the rhubarb until it's soft. The balsamic vinegar and black pepper give the sauce a little bite.

3	large egg yolks
½	cup plus 2 tablespoons sugar
1	cup milk
½	cup frozen orange juice concentrate
½	cup golden raisins
½	cup coarsely chopped pistachios
4	tablespoons unsalted butter
1	10-ounce box instant couscous
2	cups diced fresh pineapple
1	pint fresh strawberries, hulled and diced
1	tablespoon balsamic vinegar
	Freshly ground black pepper to taste

First make a crème anglaise: Beat the egg yolks and ½ cup sugar in a bowl with a whisk until the mixture turns pale and thick and ribbons form. Heat the milk until it is warm but not boiling and add the milk to the yolk, stirring constantly. Transfer the mixture to a saucepan and cook over low heat, stirring constantly, until the custard just coats the spoon, about 15 minutes.

In a separate small saucepan, reduce the orange juice concentrate by half over high heat. Add the juice to the crème anglaise and stir well.

In a skillet, briefly sauté the raisins and pistachios in 2 tablespoons of the butter over medium heat. Add the couscous, stirring all the time to make sure it doesn't brown, and cook for 2 minutes more. Add the crème anglaise and stir to blend. Let sit for 30 minutes to allow the couscous to soften, then pack the mixture tightly into lightly buttered ½-cup ramekins. If you wish to make the recipe to this point, cover and refrigerate. (Before serving, bring the ramekins to room temperature or heat in the microwave on high power for 1 minute.)

In the same skillet wiped clean, melt the remaining butter over low heat, add the fruit and remaining sugar, and cook until the sugar has melted and the fruit is just soft, about 3 minutes. Sprinkle on the vinegar and add a few grinds of pepper.

Divide the fruit among 6 dessert plates and unmold the contents of a couscous-filled ramekin at the center of each plate. Serve at once.

TUSCAN FIG AND BREAD TART

SERVES 6 TO 8

The taste of the sweet figs and rosemary together is quite unforgettable. This is actually a dessert version of the classic Italian egg and cheese strata. Moved to morning, it makes a delicious breakfast treat. Try varying the recipe by using walnut bread or brioche instead of the country loaf.

⅓ cup golden raisins
2 tablespoons Grand Marnier liqueur
1 loaf day-old Italian or French peasant-type bread, cut into ½-inch slices, about 12 slices
3 cups milk
⅓ cup plus 2 tablespoons sugar
1 pound ripe fresh figs, halved
2 tablespoons finely chopped fresh rosemary
Zest of 1 lemon
4 large eggs
1 cup heavy cream
Pinch of salt
1 tablespoon unsalted butter

Place the raisins in a small bowl and pour the Grand Marnier over them. Let stand for 30 minutes.

Place the bread slices in a single layer in a shallow roasting pan or baking dish and pour 2 cups of the milk over them. Let stand for 30 minutes, then gently squeeze as much milk as possible from the slices without tearing them. Reserve the milk.

Preheat the oven to 375°F. Butter a 12- by 14-inch baking dish. Dust with 1 tablespoon sugar.

Place the bread in a single layer in the baking dish. Cover with the fig halves, cut side down. Sprinkle the raisins and their liquid, the rosemary, and the lemon zest over the figs.

Beat together the remaining 1 cup milk, the reserved milk from soaking the bread, the eggs, cream, ⅓ cup sugar, and salt. Pour this mixture evenly over the tart.

SUN-DRIED TOMATO AND

GRUYÈRE CHEESE PUFFS

•

VEGETARIAN CASSOULET

•

MUSHROOM SALAD

•

TUSCAN FIG AND

BREAD TART

WINE SUGGESTIONS:
A MEDIUM-BODIED CALIFORNIA
ZINFANDEL OR A CHIANTI
CLASSICO RISERVA

Sprinkle with the remaining tablespoon of sugar, dot with butter, and bake for 45 minutes to 1 hour or until puffy and browned. Serve warm or at room temperature.

Black Sesame Tuiles

These thin, crisp cookies named for their resemblance to curved roof tiles (*tuiles*) are perfect foils for ice cream, sorbet, or fresh fruit compote. This is another recipe inspired by the gifted chef/owners of the Wappo Bistro and Grill in Calistoga, California. Michelle Mutrux and Aaron Bauman make their tuiles with toasted sesame seeds; I like the dramatic look of black sesame seeds.

You will need parchment paper to bake these. Michelle's homemade version of cooking spray leads off the recipe to facilitate the removal of the delicate cookies from the paper.

Glazing the Parchment Paper

¼	pound (1 stick) unsalted butter
½	cup all-purpose flour

Tuiles

2	ounces sesame seeds
2½	ounces black sesame seeds*
⅔	cup sugar
¾	cup all-purpose flour
2	tablespoons unsalted butter, melted
	Pinch of salt
1	cup egg whites, about 8 medium eggs, separated

To make the glaze, melt the butter in a small saucepan and stir in the flour to make a smooth paste. Line several baking sheets with parchment paper and brush the paper all over with the butter-flour mixture.

Preheat the oven to 375°F.

To make the tuiles, combine the sesame seeds, sugar, flour, and melted butter in a mixing bowl and stir to blend. Add the salt and egg whites and beat until well mixed.

Drop batter by the tablespoon several inches apart on the prepared parchment paper. Using a 1-inch spatula or table knife, spread the mixture thinly into ovals of approximately 3 by 4 inches.

Bake for 10 to 12 minutes or until evenly brown. Working quickly, immediately roll each cookie into a cylindrical, or cigarette, shape or drape over a rolling pin until crisp. If the cookies become too brittle to roll, return them to the oven for a few minutes to soften. (Bake only one baking sheet at a time so the cookies don't burn or become too brittle while you're working with them.) The cookies should be eaten the same day they are made.

Variation: For Coconut and Lime Tuiles, substitute ⅓ cup unsweetened coconut for the sesame seeds and add 1 tablespoon grated lime zest.

*Crisper in texture and earthier in flavor than white or beige sesame, the black sesame seeds popular in Chinese and Japanese cooking have strong visual appeal when scattered on salads and other dishes. Penzey's Spice House (P.O. Box 1488, Waukesha, WI 53187; 414-574-0277) is a good source for them and for hundreds of other whole and ground spices, often sold well below supermarket prices.

Zucchini Cake with Fruit and Nuts

MAKES ONE 1-POUND LOAF CAKE

This is an excellent cake to have with fresh strawberries or just lightly toasted and spread with ricotta or cream cheese for breakfast.

     Butter and flour for the pan
10 **tablespoons unsalted butter, melted**
4 **medium eggs, beaten**
1 **cup sugar**
1 **teaspoon vanilla extract**
2 **cups all-purpose flour**
1 **teaspoon salt**
½ **teaspoon cinnamon**
1½ **teaspoons baking powder**
2 **cups firmly packed grated zucchini, about 3 medium zucchini**
½ **cup walnuts**
½ **cup golden raisins**
1 **tablespoon finely grated lemon zest**

Preheat the oven to 350°F. Lightly butter and flour a 1-pound loaf pan.

In a bowl, blend together the butter, eggs, sugar, and vanilla.

In a separate bowl, mix the flour, salt, cinnamon, and baking powder; add the dry ingredients to the butter mixture and beat until smooth. Add the grated zucchini, walnuts, raisins, and lemon zest and stir until well blended. Pour into the prepared pan and bake for 1 hour or until a toothpick inserted in the center comes out clean.

Cool the cake in the pan for 10 minutes before turning it out onto a rack. Serve warm or at room temperature. Carefully wrapped in plastic, the cake will keep for several days.

LAVENDER SHORTBREADS

MAKES ABOUT 2½ DOZEN COOKIES

Lavender gives these shortbreads a haunting taste. The cookies are lovely with summer ices or ice creams or on their own with a glass of dessert wine. I like to slice fresh peaches into some dessert wine or champagne and eat the cookies and fruit with my fingers and finally drink the peach-scented wine. Rosemary shortbreads are equally good. Make a batch of each.

Purplish blue lavender blossoms are one of the essential *herbes de Provence*. If you can't grow your own, look for the dried buds in spice, herbal, or gourmet stores. Perhaps the easiest source is Mountain Rose Herbs, which will mail-order you top-quality lavender in 4-ounce, 8-ounce, or 1-pound bags (P.O. Box 2000, Redway, CA 95560; 800-879-3337).

¼   **cup sugar**
2   **tablespoons finely chopped fresh lavender flower spikes**
       or 1 tablespoon dried lavender flowers
¼   **pound (1 stick) unsalted butter**
1½ **cups all-purpose flour**

Combine the sugar and lavender and store the mixture in a closed jar for up to 1 week. You may combine these ingredients right on the spot, but the pungent herbal flavor will not be as pronounced.

Preheat the oven to 325°F.

Cream the butter and lavender sugar until smooth. Work in the flour to make a soft ball. Press the dough into an 8-inch round or square baking pan to a thickness of ¼ inch. Prick all over with a fork.

Bake for 20 to 25 minutes, until the shortbread is just turning golden around the edges. Cool for 5 minutes, then cut into squares or triangles.

Wrapped tightly, the cookies will keep for a week, or they can be frozen.

ESCAROLE-SHALLOT-APPLE

TARTE TATIN

•

FARCI WITH FRESH

WHITE CHEESE

•

PARSLEY AND MINT SALAD

•

CARROTS WITH ANISEED

•

FRESH FRUIT WITH

GOOD SPIRITS

•

LAVENDER SHORTBREADS

WINE SUGGESTIONS:
A FRESH WHITE WINE FROM
HAUTE-SAVOIE OR AN
OREGON PINOT GRIS

Peach and Blueberry Buckle

The spongy batter beneath the peaches and blueberries buckles upward in the baking. Perhaps this is what distinguishes buckles from cobblers, crumbles, crisps, grunts, roly-polies, pandowdies, and all the host of homey fruit and pastry desserts of English origin whose names attest to the affectionate place they hold in our hearts. They are among my very favorite desserts.

Butter for the baking dish

Batter

¼	**cup unsalted butter**
⅓	**cup sugar**
1	**large egg, beaten**
	Pinch of salt
1½	**teaspoons baking powder**
1	**cup all-purpose flour**
⅓	**cup milk**

Filling

1	**pound ripe peaches, peeled, pitted, and cut into chunks**
1½	**cups blueberries, washed, about ¾ pound**
2	**tablespoons sugar or to taste**
½	**teaspoon ground cinnamon**

Topping:

½	**cup unsalted butter**
½	**cup sugar**
½	**cup all-purpose flour**
½	**teaspoon ground cinnamon**
⅛	**teaspoon ground ginger**
⅛	**teaspoon freshly grated nutmeg**

Olive Mousse

•

Savory Wine Biscuits

•

Vegetable Risotto with Carrot, Celery, and Parsley Broth

•

Peach and Blueberry Buckle

Wine suggestions:
A Chianti Classico Riserva or a California Sangiovese

Preheat the oven to 350°F. Butter a 10-inch-diameter baking dish at least 2 inches deep.

To make the batter, combine the butter and sugar in a mixing bowl and beat until smooth. Add the egg and beat well. In a separate bowl, sift together the salt, baking powder, and flour, then add the dry ingredients to the butter and egg mixture. Add the milk and blend well. Spread the batter in the prepared baking dish.

For the filling, mix the peaches, blueberries, sugar, and cinnamon together in a separate bowl. Spread over the batter.

For the topping, combine all the ingredients and rub them together until crumbly. Sprinkle the topping over the fruit mixture.

Bake for 40 to 45 minutes or until the batter is cooked through and the fruit bubbling. Serve warm or at room temperature with cream, ice cream, or yogurt if you wish.

RHUBARB COBBLER

SERVES 8

WINE SUGGESTIONS:
A CALIFORNIA SAUVIGNON
BLANC OR BLANC DE NOIR
SPARKLING WINE

Pretty and pink, this old-fashioned dessert is especially good in spring, when the rhubarb is young and tender (the brightly colored base of fresh-cut stalks is tastiest of all). Golden raisins add texture as well as sweetness.

Butter for the baking dish
4 **cups chopped rhubarb in 1-inch lengths**
½ **cup golden raisins**
½ **cup lightly toasted almond slivers**
1 **cup packed light brown sugar**
4 **tablespoons unsalted butter**
2 **large eggs, lightly beaten**
½ **cup milk**
1½ **cups all-purpose flour**
2 **teaspoons baking powder**
1 **teaspoon vanilla extract**
1 **cup granulated sugar**

Preheat the oven to 350°F. Grease a 9- by 11-inch baking dish with butter.

In a medium bowl, combine the rhubarb, raisins, almonds, and brown sugar. Mix well and set aside.

Melt 3 tablespoons of the butter. In a large bowl, combine the melted butter, eggs, milk, flour, baking powder, vanilla, and granulated sugar. Beat until smooth.

Pour the batter into the prepared dish. Spread the rhubarb mixture over the batter and gently press it down so that most of the fruit is buried in the batter. Dot with the remaining tablespoon of butter. Bake for 45 minutes or until a cake tester inserted into the center comes out clean.

Serve warm with vanilla ice cream, sweetened yogurt, or crème fraîche.

When Less Is More: Fruit Combined with Wine or Spirits for Elegant Finales

I am always relieved when a dinner party dessert turns out to be a simple fruit dessert, particularly after a dinner of epic proportions. It takes sophistication and culinary confidence to pass up the flourish of a chocolate-decadence-style dessert when capping off a great evening. Don't get me wrong; I adore the gooey drop-dead desserts as much as anyone—but not after a heavy meal. In my opinion these extravaganzas are best reserved for late afternoon or for late in the evening after a movie or some other post-prandial activity or event.

Mellow fruit with wine—or liqueur or brandy—is the very best finale for a rich meal. Fresh in-season fruit is my favorite, but for those times when fresh fruit is either scarce or of poor quality, dried fruit macerated in a complementary wine or spirit makes a surprisingly good substitute.

Fruit and wine are natural allies (think grapes), and the felicitous combinations are many. Add a spice or herbal note and you invite an intriguing subtlety. Fresh and vibrant on their own, these desserts go well with a simple cookie or a scoop of sorbet or even ice cream.

Here are some matchups:

Fresh Fruit with Good Spirits

For every pound of fruit you will need about 2 cups of poaching liquid. In a nonreactive saucepan, heat the wine or spirit for 5 minutes with up to 1 tablespoon of chopped fresh herbs that you wish to use. Put the fruit in a heatproof bowl and pour the wine over it. Cool to room temperature or chill. For a sweeter version, add up to 1 cup of sugar for every 2 cups of liquid. For a concentrated syrup, remove the fruit and reduce the syrup over high heat by half.

For your garnishes, choose from mint, lemon verbena, scented geranium leaves, basil, or zest of lime or orange. A grind of freshly ground pepper is also good.

SHREDDED ZUCCHINI SALAD

•

GRILLED TUNA WITH SAFFRON

VINAIGRETTE

•

GOAT CHEESE CAKE AND SALAD

OF MIXED GREENS

•

FRESH FRUIT WITH

GOOD SPIRITS

•

LAVENDER SHORTBREADS

WINE SUGGESTIONS:
A FRENCH POUILLY-FUMÉ OR A
MEDIUM-BODIED CALIFORNIA
SAUVIGNON BLANC

WARM BEET SALAD WITH
WALNUTS AND DILL

•

SFORMATO OF CAULIFLOWER
WITH TOMATO-WATERCRESS
CONCASSÉE

•

SFORMATO OF CARROTS

•

CHIVE POPOVERS

•

FRESH FRUIT WITH
GOOD SPIRITS

WINE SUGGESTIONS:
ROSSO DI MONTALCINO OR A
CALIFORNIA SANGIOVESE OR A
LIGHT- TO MEDIUM-BODIED
ZINFANDEL

- Strawberries, raspberries, blackberries, or plums with Grand Marnier, cassis, framboise, or Chartreuse
- Cherries with Amaretto
- Peaches or nectarines with Amaretto, Vin Santo, Frangelico, or Sauternes
- Cranberries or rhubarb stewed in best-quality blackberry wine
- Pears with poire, Amaretto, or port
- Grapes with grappa
- Apples, pears, or bananas with cognac, Armagnac, or bourbon whiskey
- Oranges, grapefruit, or kumquats with late-harvest Riesling
- Mangoes, papayas, or pineapple with dark Jamaican rum
- Melon with port

Melon with Port

This is the perfect dessert for a picnic. Take no dishes; the melon halves act as bowls. Oh so simple.

3   **small ripe Charentais or other orange-fleshed melons at room temperature**
¾   **cup ruby port**

Cut the melons in half and discard the seeds. Pour about 2 tablespoons of port into the cavity of each melon half and serve.

Dried Fruit with Good Spirits

For every ¾ pound of dried fruit you will need 2 cups of poaching liquid. In a nonreactive saucepan, heat the wine or spirit with up to 1 tablespoon of chopped fresh herbs or spices for 5 minutes. For a sweeter version, add up to 1 cup of sugar for every 2 cups of liquid. Add the dried fruit and poach only until the fruit swells up and is tender. The time will vary from 2 to 10 minutes, depending on the size of the fruit. Cool in the syrup or serve warm. For a more concentrated version, remove the fruit and reduce the syrup over high heat by half.

Add star anise, bay leaf, stick cinnamon, nutmeg, allspice, juniper berries, or freshly grated lemon, lime, or orange zest while cooking. Garnish with chopped, lightly toasted nuts.

- Raisins with grappa
- Figs, raisins, dates, or prunes with late-harvest Riesling
- Pears, apricots, berries (blueberries, strawberries, cranberries), cherries, and/or dried citron with late-harvest Riesling, full-bodied red wine, port, whiskey, dark Jamaican rum, or a whisper of orange-flower or rose water.

MINTED SNOW PEA AND

POTATO SOUP

•

WILD MUSHROOM

SALLY LUNN

•

HOT-SWEET COLESLAW WITH

CARAMELIZED ALMONDS

•

PERFECT GINGERBREAD

•

DRIED FRUIT WITH

GOOD SPIRITS

WINE SUGGESTIONS:
A CALIFORNIA VIOGNIER OR
PINOT BLANC

The following recipe from the inimitable *Gold and Fizdale Cookbook* captures perfectly the spirit of these elegant less-is-more desserts.

A Raisin Nightcap

For nondessert-eaters or as a novel after-dinner liqueur.

Put heaped tablespoons of seedless raisins in small glasses. Fill the glasses three-quarters full with grappa, Marc de Bourgone, or Calvados. Let the raisins soak for several hours. Serve with demitasse spoons.

Eat the liqueur-soaked raisins and then sip the raisin-flavored liqueur. Heady and delicious!

From Arthur Gold and Robert Fizdale, *The Gold and Fizdale Cookbook* (Random House, 1984).

Index

274 Index